THE PENGUIN POETS

AS WE KNOW

John Ashbery was born in Rochester, New York, in 1927, grew up on a farm in western New York State, and was educated at Deerfield Academy, Harvard, and Columbia, where he specialized in English literature. In 1955 he went to France, where he wrote art criticism for the Paris *Herald Tribune*. He returned to New York in 1965, was Executive Editor of *Art News* until 1972, and now teaches English at Brooklyn College. He is also the art critic for *New York* magazine. His books of poetry include *Turandot and Other Poems, Some Trees, The Tennis Court Oath, Rivers and Mountains, The Double Dream of Spring, Three Poems,* and, most recently, *Houseboat Days*. He has written plays and essays and is coauthor, with James Schuyler, of a novel, *A Nest of Ninnies*. He was awarded the Pulitzer Prize, the National Book Award, and the National Book Critics Circle Award for *Self-Portrait in a Convex Mirror. Three Poems, Houseboat Days,* and *Self-Portrait in a Convex Mirror* are published by Penguin Books.

AS WE KNOW

POEMS BY
JOHN ASHBERY

PENGUIN BOOKS

Penguin Books Ltd, Harmondsworth, Middlesex, England
Penguin Books, 40 West 23rd Street,
New York, New York 10010, U.S.A.
Penguin Books Australia Ltd, Ringwood, Victoria, Australia
Penguin Books Canada Limited, 2801 John Street,
Markham, Ontario, Canada L3R 1B4
Penguin Books (N.Z.) Ltd, 182–190 Wairau Road,
Auckland 10, New Zealand

First published in the United States of America in simultaneous hardcover
and paperback editions by The Viking Press and Penguin Books 1979
Reprinted 1980, 1986

LIBRARY OF CONGRESS CATALOGING IN PUBLICATION DATA
Ashbery, John.
As we know.
I. Title.
PS3501.S475A9 1978   811'.5'4   79-17246
ISBN 0 14 058.5915

Printed in the United States of America by
American Book–Stratford Press, Inc., Saddle Brook, New Jersey
Set in CRT Electra

Grateful acknowledgment is made to the following publications, in
which these poems first appeared: *American Poetry Review*: "Litany"
(Part II). *Broadway*: "Otherwise." *Cincinnati Poetry Review*: "And I'd
Love You to Be in It." *Contemporary Poets Calendar* (1980): "A Tone
Poem." *Harvard Magazine*: "The Picnic Grounds" and "Their Day."
New York Review of Books: "My Erotic Double" and "*Histoire Uni-
verselle.*" *The New Yorker*: "Haunted Landscape," "Knocking Around,"
and "Tapestry." *Paris Review*: "Homesickness" and "This Configura-
tion." *Ploughshares*: "No, But I Seen One You Know You Don't
Own," "The Shower," "Landscapeople," and "The Plural of 'Jack-in-
the-Box'" (as part of the sequence "*Kannst du die alten Lieder noch
Spielen?*"). *Poetry*: "Many Wagons Ago," "The Sun," "Five Pedantic
Pieces," "Flowering Death," "Not only /but also," "Train Rising out
the Sea," and "Late Echo." *Vogue*: "As We Know." *The World*:
"Sleeping in the Corners of Our Lives" and "In a Boat." *Zero*: "Varia-
tions on an Original Theme" and "The Other Cindy."

"The Preludes," "A Box and Its Contents," "A Sparkler," "The Wine,"
"There's No Difference," "Hittite Lullaby," "No, But I Seen One You
Know You Don't Own," "The Shower," "Landscapeople," and "The
Plural of 'Jack-in-the-Box'" appear in *Solitary Travelers*, a volume of
Mellon Lectures published by Cooper Union.

CONTENTS

I ❋ LITANY

AUTHOR'S NOTE

The two columns of "Litany" are meant to be read as simultaneous but independent monologues.

I

For someone like me
The simple things
Like having toast or
Going to church are
Kept in one place.

Like having wine and cheese.
The parents of the town
Pissing elegantly escape knowledge
Once and for all. The
Snapdragons consumed in a wind
Of fire and rage far over
The streets as they end.

The casual purring of a donkey
Rouses me from my accounts:
What given, what gifts. The air
Stands straight up like a tail.

He spat on the flowers.

Also for someone
Like me the time flows round again
With things I did in it.
I wish to keep my differences

I

So this must be a hole
Of cloud
Mandate or trap
But haze that casts
The milk of enchantment

Over the whole town,
Its scenery, whatever
Could be happening
Behind tall hedges
Of dark, lissome knowledge.

The brown lines persist
In explicit sex
Matters like these
No one can care about,
"Noone." That is I've said it
Before and no one
Remembers except that elf.

Around us are signposts
Pointing to the past,
The old-fashioned, pointed
Wooden kind. And nothing directs
To the present that is

And to retain my kinship
To the rest. That is why
I raise these flowers all around.
They do not stand for flowers or
Anything pretty they are
Code names for the silence.

And just as it
Always keeps getting sorted out
And there is still the same amount to do
I wish to remain happily among these islands
Of rabbit-eared leaved plants
And sand and lava rock
That is so little tedious.
My way shall run from there
And not mind the pain
Of getting there. This is an outburst.

The last rains fed
Into the newly opened canal.

The dust blows in.
The disturbance is
Nonverbal communication:
Meaningless syllables that
Have a music of their own,
The music of sex, or any
Nameless event, something
That can only be taken as
Itself. This rules ideas
Of what else may be there,

About to happen.

These traumas
That sped us on our way
Are to be linked with the invisible damage
Resulting in the future
From too much direction,
Too many coils
Of remembrance, too much arbitration.
And the sun shines
On all of it
Fairly and equitably.
It was a way of getting to see the world
At minimal cost and without
Risk
But it can no longer stand up to
That.

The fences are barrel staves
Surrounding, encroaching on
The pattern of the city,
The formula that once made sense to
A few of us until it became
The end.

The magic has left the
Drawings finally.
They blow around the rest—tumbleweed
In a small western ghost town
That sometimes hits and sometimes misses.

Which regroup farther on,
Standing around looking at
The hole left by the great implosion.
It is they who carry news of it
To other places. Therefore
Are they not the event itself?

Especially since it persists
In dumbness which isn't even
A negative articulation—persists
And collapses into itself.

I had greatly admired
The shirt.
He looks fairly familiar.

The pancake
Is around in idea.
Today the wisteria is in league
With the Spanish minstrels.

Who come to your house
To serenade it
All or in part.

The windows are open again
The dust blows through
A diagram of a room.
This is where it all
Had to take place,

That tower of lightning high over
The Sahara Desert could have missed you,
An experience
Unlike any other, leaching
Back into the lore of
The songs and sagas,
The warp of knowledge.
But now it's
Come close
Strict identities form it,
Build it up like sheaves
Of nerves, articulate,
Defiant of itself.

The posse had seen them
Pass by like a caravan
In slow motion,
Elephants and wolves
Painted bright colors,
Hardly visible
Through the cistern of shade
Of a hand held up to the eye.

Now that they are gone and
To be dreamed of
A new alertness changes
Into the look of things
Placed on the railing
Of this terrace:
The beheld with all the potential

Around a drum of living,
The motion by which a life
May be known and recognized,
A shipwreck seen from the shore,
A puzzling column of figures.
The dark shirt dragged frequently
Through the bayou.

Your luggage
Is found
Upon the plane.

If I could plan how
To remember what had indeed once
Been there
Without reference to professions,
Medical school,
Etc.,
Being there indeed once
(Everyday occurrence),
We stopped at the Pacific Airport
To hear the rush of disguises
For the elegant truth, notwithstanding
Some in underwear stood around
Puddles in the darkened
Cement and sodium lights
Beyond the earthworks
Beyond the chain-link fence
Until dawn touched with her cool
Stab of grace nobody deserved (but
It's always that way isn't it)

Of the visible, acting
To release itself
Into the known
Dust under
The sky.

Hands where it took place
Moving over the nebulous
Keyboard: the heft
Now invisible, only the fragments
Of the echo are left
Intruding into the color,
How we remember them.

How quickly the years pass
To next year's sun
In the mountain family.

All the barriers are loaded
With fruit and flowers
At the same time.
The leaves stumble up to
Intercept the light one last time
Outnumbering the sheaves,
Even the ants on the anthill,
Black line leading to
The cake of disasters,
Leading outward to encircle the profit
Of laughter and ending of all the tales
In an explosion of surprise and marbled
Opinions as the sun closes in

Le charme du matin
You and Sven-Bertil must
At some point have overridden
The barriers real or fancied
Blowing like bedcurtains later
In the oyster light—
Something I saw once
Reminded me of it:
That old, evil, not-so-secret
Formula
Now laundered, made to look
Transparent. Surely
There is a shoulder there,
Some high haunch half-sketched, a tremor
And intent to the folds that shower from the sky.

And must
At some earlier time
Seem the garter
The cow in the trees.

What was green before
Is homeless.
The mica on the front
Of the prefecture spells out
"Coastline"—a speedboat
Would alter even at a distance
But they shift anyway
Come round
To my idea
My hat

Building darkness.

In later editions you
Were called casual, harsh,
Dispensing arbitrary edicts
Under present law
Timed and always sunk in the
Gnat-embroiled shade.
It was in fact a colossal
Desert full of valleys and
Melting canyons and soared
Under the heaving of sighs
Knowing it would all end
But never end, but exist
In the memory of itself turned to flesh
Of ice cream and sting
Without obliteration.

But as I see it you
Can only amble on, not free
Nor on a journey, appearing
Though at some later
Juncture
Of our tepid and insidious
Greeting:
The shock of the path
Worn like this
Never scaled
Beyond a certain point
And returning and returning
Like a pole pointed to the sky.

As it would be
If I were you
In dreams and in business
Only, in supper meetings
On the general line of progress
If I had a talking picture of you.

You are
So perversely evasive:
The ticking of a clock in the
Background could be
Only the plait.

We must learn to read
In the dark, to enjoy the long hills
Of studious celebrity.
The long Chinese shadow that
Hooks over a little
At the top
The stone that sinks
To the bottom of the aquarium:
All this mummified writing
As the dusting of new light
In the hollow collar of a hill
That never completes its curve
Or the thought of what
It was going to say: our going in.

The hedges are nice and it's too bad
That one bad axe stroke could fell
Whatever needed to advertise its

In some Greek
Coves barely under the water
Or barely inundated (you might say)
A ball was found, and stated
The body's predilection to it:
There is no more history you
Seem to say no more June.
The blue wraith that stands
Straight above each chimney: forget it!
It is almost gone,
Has almost departed.
Now the dry, half-seen pods
Are layered, and the beating
Of an old man in some dungeon.
No one sees how fast its processes
Whiz, until some day
When things are better.

Who can elicit these possible,
Rubbery spirals? Return of all that's new,
Antithesis chirping
To antithesis: let's climb
The roof, look out over all
That was so near and is:
Vanity of the dishpan,
The radio chortling succor to moved
Behemoths of sense shredding
Underwear and ulcers alike
In a past of no mean confection:
This wound like a small wall

Very existence.
And then cars strut forth on the highway
Singly and in groups
Of three and four: orange,
Flamingo, blue-pencil blue,
The gray of satisfaction, the red
Of discussion, and now, moved, the sky
Calls itself up.

As leaves are seen in mirrors
In libraries
Half-noticed, the sound
Half-remembered and the
Continuing chapter half-sketched—
O were we wrong to notice
To remember so much
When so little else has survived?

All were moments big with particulars
An elaborate pastry concocted in the wings
In darkness, and each
Has vanished on the carrousel
Of rage, along the coast
Like a chameleon's hide.
The suffering, the pleasure that broke
Over it like a wave,
Are these fixed limits, off-limits
To the game as darkness confounds
The two teams, makes it one with chance?
Still, somewhere wings are
Being slowly lifted,

Of ceramic intent:
It is meant to hound you
With its brothers in the afterlight
Of forest prisms, the brown sky sweeping
Unusually
Away. The cavern this time is big enough to fit in:
The broken apse
Wind slams through, the snail-sexton
With rheumy specs, dung beetle bringing up the rear:
Who could explain it?
Who could have explained it?
"Only pluralism . . ." but we get
Far less for our money that way.
Aye, and fewer replies too
To sopping prayer-strips
Hanging like dejected plumage from that
Rafter over the porch swing.
They are anxious to be done with us,
For the interview to be over, and we,
We have just begun.

Yet I too
Was once captured this way.
How it became a delight
To think about it and when
Pain intervened, as usual,
The calm remained, held over
From the other time
And no broken trace was seen.

Now houses have been razed

Over and over again.

The point must have been made.

But out of so much color
It still does come again
The colors of tiger lilies and around
And down, remembered
Now as dirty colors, the color
Of forgetting-grass, of
Old rags or sleep, buoyed
On the small zephyrs
That keep the hour and remind each boy
To turn home from school past the sheep
In the paper meadow and to wind the clock.
An old round is being passed out,
The players take their places.
How nice that in the stalls
Is still room for certain boys to stand,
The main song is successfully
Programmed and the others too in part:
Enough gets through to make the occasion
A glottal one full of success
And coated with the film of success
In which are reflected
Many a bright occasion
Lads who go out with girls
In the numb prime of springtime
For instance.
Except for that, the camera sighs,
Is no hollow behind the black backing.

Where once fields of vegetables
Stood; nothing's there
That cannot truly be
And was all along
Yet never was for the seeing,
The tasting that jabs back
Into the past as well,
For what is present savoring?
Mouthing of initials, of a career?
There is no case
For samurai, or witches' coattails,
But so long as the buoyant opening
Of a vacant career stand around healthily
There is no need to ascertain
The pink and red paper stratosphere
Balloons pasted a little crazily
Against a teetering sky
Where color cannot have ever been.

There was another photograph
In that album, but not so amusing
To remember or to describe:
Three dark women
On a swerving path that saucily
Pulled the rug out from under the spectator.
And the three expressions faded or
Were never there to begin with, picking
Up a little strength perhaps from the exhausted
Eye that watched them, guardedly.
And all it said was, we are stones
To be like this and never to be able

That was short-lived.
A sheaf of selected odes
Bundled on the waters.

A superior time
Of blueberries and passion flowers,
Of a four-poster.
The thirties light
Has infested the blond
Hairdo from the grooves up
But we must not treasure
It less in the magnesium
Flare that is manna to all things
In the here and now. You were saying
How she is coming along, praying
For it to be better
Day by day.

And some of these days the waning
Silver lashes out
Like a trussed alligator:
Mother and the kids standing around
The bowl that is portal,
Hitching post, tufted
Mattress and field of wild
Scruffy flowers are removed
One by one as a demonstration.
See, there is only light.
Nothing to live at,
To worry.

To reveal, being forward like this, but we can say
How repellent was the adumbration
That lodged us here, around
Our holes, and did not
Shove us away, but rather
As with brave looks out to sea
Left everything here to crumble,
Whether new and fine, or old
Or like us, not new nor old
Having no share in the time-cusp
That keeps you and they running here to imagined
Meetings as though some sense were here
In the fences and the privileged
Omissions of the frolic grass.

A close one.
I haven't seen him
Since I've been here.
Only an aftertaste of medicine
And subtle pressures put
Beyond this lattice that is
As narrow as the visible universe.

A whisper directs:
How many homeless,
Wandering, improvisatory
As new deserts move up
Into the constellation that was
Only a moment ago.
Straggling players reverse
The indications:

It is the old sewer of our resources
Disguised again as a corridor.
There is some anthropology here
It seems, and then
The dust on the jamb is warning
And intrigue enough. The summer day is put by.
The bells in the shower
Are outnumbered by plain queries
Whose answer is their falling echo.

Birds in modish, corporeal
Gear take off at the
Scallops of the umbrella.
This past is sampled and is again
The right one, and in testing
For the zillionth time we are
As built into the fixed wall of water
That indicates where the present leaves off
And the past begins, whose transparencies
Admit impressions of traceries of leaves
And shallow birds among memories.

The climate seceded then,
The glad speculation about what clothes
They wore stacked like leaves,
Speckled behind the eye of what
Consumer, what listener?
And the praise is lascivious
To the onyx ear at evening
But not forwarded

Lutes, feathers, hard
Leather berries fall:
The autumn in the spring
Again with July sandwiched
In the middle, lament
Of all the days from the least popular
To the most sought after, the play
Forever turning on itself:

Refrains, the spirit of sorrow
Begin it; duration
Only conjugates, the last happening
Is seen as inadequate only after the passing
Of much else varied stuff.
Only in being turned inside out
Can it deny itself so that the meaning
Pierces in any given point
And in the texture of the sea, O
Sky-blue-violet raiment given
Not to be heeded
Only as an oblique arch through which sails
Perpendicular
The speeding hollow bullet of these times
Of mud and velvet, these
Choreographed intrusions.
Farther from far away
No more the colored echoes ring
On the afternoon groundswell already dissolved
In the thousands of hastening
Feet of birds and raindrops
In wasted penitence sucked back

Into the ring with the other shouting,
The desperate competitions willed
Until darkness, dripping toward death
By late morning.
She circles plainly away
From it in wider and wider loops,
And what have you to say? What account
To give? Of the season's vast
Storehouse of agendas, bales
Of items for discussion dwindling
Down to a last seed on the stone doorstep?
If this was the season only of death
That licorice blast would not keep only
In its retelling the unfurled
Question-mark of the shaved future but redound
To us waiting here against the spike fence
In pleasant attitudes from which the waiting
Is forgotten like thorns in the memory
Of laced paths merging on
Extinct, ultimate slopes,
But trap us in the game of two flavors
(A rising shout some distance away,
The tabac alike in resisting
Terribilità
Yet basing it on us, all the same
A knowledge of its measure, its
Proportion, until the end is sought
Dryly, among stringent grasses).
To have sought it any more, mining
Its anfractuosities, is to bear witness,
The living getting trampled

Up to the crest again
From which the view is fine as views go
From low, stubby towers
Of which there aren't too many
Here
Like cash registers in a darkened store
Even as a fresh dawn approaches, before
The winds come.

Further on up only birches
Grow and the red sweater
Is for you. You breathing
Into the angle of shadow in sunlight
Of the frosted kiosk that was taken
By men with tools and a surveying kit.
That was long after
The night out on the glacier.

In the morning the children and kittens ran around.

It wasn't necessary to remind us
Once we were seated at our desks in the school
Under the giant tree-roots sheathed
In moss about the quartz lightning
Tumbling down the bed of the stream
As on a stair. We were quick and ready
For level plant-games in the sun
That arrived just at noon as a horizontal line.
The error was in the hollowed-out, weed-choked
Afternoon and even it was only confession
Of too many strands of vagueness, neuters

Underfoot always the same way
And as surely one desiccated spike of
Sea-oats rises quizzically after the
Hordes have passed over, the film
Slips over the cogs
That brought us to this unearthly spot.
So death is really an appetite for time
That can see through the haze of blue
Smoke-rings to the turquoise ceiling.
She said this once and turned away
Knowing we wanted to hear it twice,
But knowing also as we knew that speculation
Raves and raves as on a mirror
To the outlandish accompaniment of its own death
That reads as life to the toilers
And potboys who make up these blond
Coils of citizenry which are life in the abstract.

What it was like to be mouthing those
Solemn abstractions that were crimson
And solid as beefsteak. One
Shouldn't be surprised by
The smell of mignonette and the loss
As each stands still, and the softness
Of the land behind each one,
Where each one comes from.
Because it is the way of the personality of each
To blush and act confused, groping
For the wrong words so that the
Coup de théâtre
Will unfold all at once like shaken-out

Too independent of each other and yet
Abashed with the other heretics like ourselves:
Clusters of black inkberries sweeping the horizon
And we always prepared for a fight
Yet so innocent we have no place to go.

The spaces between the teeth told you
That the smile hung like an aria on the mind
And all effort came into being
Only to yank it away
Came at it
Hard as the lines of citrus planted
In firm yet wavering rows
All across the land to the water.

Bells were rung
For some members of the family only,
These relatives like scarlet trees who infested
The background but were not much more than
The dust as it is seen
In folds of the furniture,
These were the ones who were always
Pushing out toward the Pacific coast—what
A time we all had of it, but all that part
Is over, in a chapter
That somehow has passed us by. And yet, I wonder.

Certainly the academy has performed
A useful function. Where else could
Tiny flecks of plaster float almost
Forever in innocuous sundown almost

14

Lightning and no one
Will have heard anything. The gray,
Fake Palladian club buildings will
Still stand the next moment, at their grim
Business: empty entablatures, *oeils-de-boeuf*,
Gun-metal laurels, the eye
Revolving slowly in the empty socket
That the bronze visor shades: there was
Never anything but this,
No footfalls on the mat-polished marble floor,
No bird-dropping, no fates, no sanctuary.
The sheet slowly rises to greet you.
The asters are reflected
Simultaneously in ruby drops of the wine
The morning after the great storm
That swept our sky away, leaving
A new muscle in its place: a relaxed, far-away
Tissue of scandal and dreams like noon smoke
Lingering above horizon roofs.
But what difference did any of it make
Woven on death's loom as indeed
All of it was though divided into
Chapters each with its ornamental
Capital at the beginning, and its polished
Sequel? You knew
You were coming to the end by the way the other
Would be beginning again, so that nobody
Was ever lonesome, and the story never
Came to its dramatic conclusion, but
Merely leveled out like linen close up
In the mirror. So that the roundness

Fashionable as the dark probes again.
An open beak is shadowed against the
Small liturgical opera this time.
It is nobody's fault. And the academy
Has saved it all for remembering.

It performs another useful function:
Pointing out the way at the beginning
When everybody giggled nervously and
Got lost against the peach-fuzz sky
Where too many nice miracles were always
Happening and the blood-colored ground
Grasped them like straws, for a minute.
There was a smoother, less ambiguous way
To be determined and its banners shook like smoke
To become an arch of the bridge
And the bridge was acknowledged in good time
But never to this day
As its echo in the sky performing to meet it
Behind invisible cataracts and cloud catalfalques
And yet, the carrion still
Steams here, the mote
Pursues the eye, and all is other and the same

Of which the rite dismantles bit by bit
The blind empathy
Of a homeland. It emerges as a firm
Enigma, burnished, filled in.

Furthermore, there was nothing like
Shadows of oranges

Was all around to be appreciated, yet somehow flat
As well, and could never be trusted
Even though the rushes slanted all one way
In the autumn wind, and the leaves
And branches tried to slant with them
In a poem of harmonious dejection, but it was
Only picture-making. Under
The intimate light of the lantern
One really felt rather than saw
The thin, terrifying edges between things
And their terrible cold breath.
And no one longed for the great generalities
These seemed to preclude. Each thought only
Of his private silence, and hungered
For the promised moment of rest.

In the new game, nothing fanciful
And abstract one step away from foggy
Reality. The series were all sisters
Back in the fifties when more of this
Sort of thing was allowed. Two could
Go on at once without special permission
And the dreams were responsible to no base
Of authority but could wander on for
Short distances into the amazing nearness
That the world seemed to be. Sometimes
We would all sing together
And at night people would take leave of each other
And go into their houses, singing.
It was a time of rain and Hawaii
And tears big as crystals. A time
Of reading and listening to the wireless.
We never should have parted, you and me.

II

I photographed all things,
All things as happening
As prelude, as prelude to the impatience
Of enormous summer nights opening
Out farther and farther, like the billowing
Of a parachute, with only that slit
Of starlight. The old, old
Wonderful story, and it's all right
As far as it goes, but impatience
Is the true ether that surrounds us.
Without it everything would be asphalt.

Now that the things of autumn
Have been sequestered too in their chain
The other part of the year become
Visible
And the summer night is like a goldfish bowl
With everything in full view, yet only parts
Are what is actually seen, and these supply
The rest. It's not like cheating
Since it *is* all there, but more like
Helping the truth along a little:
The artifice lets it become itself,
Nestling in truth. These are long days
And we need all the help we can get.

II

Something I read once
In some poem reminded me of it:
The dark, wet street
(It gets dark at seven now)
Gleaming, ecstatic, with the thin spear
Of faerie trumpet-calls. A lullaby
That is an exclamation.

It cannot be found
As when the whole sky shifts and stays
Where it is until the next time.
Like a summer job in a department store
It stays on and on,
Breaking up the moments, hiding
The kissing,
Taking whatever is there away from us.
Its temperature is darkness,
Its taste, the silent, bitter welcome
On the edge of the forest
When you were starting to reach home.

Also, too much is written
About it, as though each time
Were starting from zero toward an imaginary
Number. No one sees it's
Just the evening news, mostly,

We are to become ashamed only much later,
Much later on, under the long bench.
And it is not like the old days
When we used to sing off-key
For hours in the rain-drenched schoolroom
On purpose. Here, whatever is forgotten
Or stored away is imbued with vitality.
Whatever is to come is too.

How can I explain?

No matter how raffish
The new clients moving slowly along,
Taking in the sights, placing bets,
There comes a time when the moment
Is full of, knows only itself.
Like a moment when a tree
Is seen to tower above everything else,
To know itself, and to know everything else
As well, but only in terms of itself
Without knowing or having a clear concept
Of itself. This is a moment
Of fast growing, of compounding myths
As fast as they can be thrown off,
Trampled under, forgotten. The moment
Not made of itself or any other
Substance we know of, reflecting
Only itself. Then there are two moments,
How can I explain?
It was as though this thing—

A translation into the light of day,
Or two fiddles scraping along
Out of kindness, you think, but
To whom? In short, any kind of tame
Manifestation against the straw
Of darkness and the darkening trees
Until the aftertaste claimed it.

Nothing here is like the
Wet, hot vigil
That loneliness erected:
There is nothing here that can be seen
The way that city could be seen,
Most precisely at night, perhaps
When thousands of tongues inspect it
And the outline of its state of mind
Tapers off hard and clear
Until the next time.
The noises in the bedroom dissolve slowly

And at last the thread holds
So that the lining adhere strictly
Or as a plumb line erected straight into the air
To stand for all vertical constructions
That chide and quietly amaze
The pale blue of the sky.

The shops here don't sell anything
One would want to buy.
It's even hard to tell exactly what
They're selling—in one, you might

More creature than person—
Lumbered at me out of the storm,
Brandishing a half-demolished beach umbrella,
So that there might be merely this thing
And me to tell about it.
It was awful. And I too have no rest
From the storm that is always something
To worry about. Really. My unworthiness
Like a loose garment or cape of some sort
Constantly sliding off the shoulders,
Around the elbows . . . I cannot keep it on,
Even as I am invisible in the eye
Of the storm, we two are blind,
And blind to the inaudible repercussions,
The strange woody aftertaste.

After that the wave came
And left no mark on the shore.
The waves advanced as the tide withdrew.
There was nothing for it but to
Retreat from the edge of the earth,
In that time, that climate expecting rain,
Behind some brackish business
On the margin intuiting cataclysms of light.
All that fall I wanted to be with you,
Tried to catch up to you in the streets
Of that time. Needless to say,
Although we were together a good part of the time
I never quite made it to the thunder.

The boy who cried "wolf" used to live there.

Find a pile of ventilators next
To a lot of cuckoo-clock parts,
Plus used government documents and stacks
Of cans of brine shrimp, and an
Extremely elegant saleslady, in
Printed chiffon, seeming to be from a different
World entirely. But that's—que voulez-vous?—
Par for the course, I guess. You
Pick up certain things here, where
You need them, and
Do without the others for the moment,
Essential though they may be.
Every collection is as notable for its gaps
As for what's there. The wisest among us
Collect gaps, knowing it's the only way
To realize a more complete collection
Than one's neighbor's. It's also cheaper
And easier to show off to advantage.
At night rain whips the collection,
The plunge, the surge of the tide
Drowns the memory of it. Only a dark field remains
But with the return of morning, the same
Familiar sticks and pieces poke
Their extremities out of the dewy mound of straw.
The collection, at least for some people,
Is still there. And it matters
To them, and to tax collectors
And taxation buffs, because
Now none of it will get lost
Any more than it already has. A
Garage can contain it.

This place of islands and slow reefs,
Like petals of mercury, that fold up
Whenever that allusion is made.
It falls off the others like
Water off piled-up stones at the base
Of a waterfall, and the petals
Curl up, injured, into themselves.
Only the frozen emphasis
On a single thing that was out of sight
When the allusion was made, remains.

We all bought tickets to the allusion
And are disappointed, of course.
But what can you do? Events have
A way of snapping off like that, like
The glassblower's striped candy canes
Of glass at a moment he knows is coming,
Is there, even. *The old,*
Wonderful story. Not yet ended.

You who approach me,
All grace and linearity,
With my new crayons I think I'll
Do a series of box-sprays—stippled
Cobalt on the gold
Of a sun-pure afternoon
In October when things change over.
There is no longer time for a line
Or rather there are no lines in the time
Of ripeness that is past,
Yet still pausing on the ridge

All
Evening I have waited for your call.
The early period was never like this.

Even birds are happier than this.
You have
No right to take something out of life
And then put it back, knowingly, beside
Its double, from whom
The original tensions unwittingly came.

The collection matures.
Amateurs flock to it, to get a look at it.
And some day the idea
Will have been removed, extracted,
From the flurry of particulars
From numbered exhibits,
And the collected will have no end.

A few always stay behind mechanically
On a glimpsed piece of scaffolding.
There are many of us to choose from:
Blowhards, barnacles, old fogeys
Rushing up from under the earth
Into the sun!

It doesn't matter that the fruit is greenish,
Or that the ill-defined sidewalks seem to lead nowhere
As long as the clock is stowed in somebody's luggage.
The round smile of celebration

Stealing into permanence.

It was all French horns
And oboes and purple vetch:
That was what it was all about, but
What it came to be came later
And other—a scene, a
Simple situation, something as
Basic as two people sitting in the sun
With no thought of the morrow, or of today,
As the whispers mingled in a choir outlining them
And we took a lesson away from this,
A lesson like a piece of cloth.
It's going to be different in the future
But now the now is what matters,
Knowing itself old, and open to vengeance,
And, in short, up to nobody's expectations
For it, as dank and empty
As an old Chevy parked under the trees
Amid dead leaves and dogshit, everybody's
Idea of what was coming true for them
Which is now burning in lava-like letters
In the sky, a piece of good news
If you agree that good news is what
Is happening at this very instant.

The California sun turned its back on us
So we chose New England and the more vibrant
Violet light of tame tempests,
Dreams of sleeping watchdogs,
And the whole house was full of people

Is always there,
Is part of the permanent scenery
Of this age's accumulation
And seeps, or drifts, only a little.
My dear yesterday,
You were ugly and full of promise
And today the delta is forming:
The water, or is it sandbars, stretching away
Almost too far for them to mean to each other
What they still mean to us.

Another thing they can do to you
Is also celebration, but of another kind:
The dance that is a brown study
Under the skylight,
The music of eternal moping
As far as it goes, since eternity
Is an eye, and some things elude the eye:
Polite gestures, timid farewells
Alongside a flooded creek in April,
The false sparkle, the finish, the edge.

These permutate, combine
In a gentle ellipse of spoken vagaries
That pester nobody, and yet
How few invitations are received!
They say they're having trouble with the mails
And so many people have moved as
We become an increasingly mobile populace
In the deep shade of a quiet trailer park
Where nobody minds waiting

Having a good time, and though
No one offered you a drink and there were no
Clean glasses and the supper
Never appeared on the table, it was
Strangely rewarding anyway.
It gave one an idea of what they thought of one:
Even the ocean that came crashing almost
Into the back yard did not seem ill-disposed
And that was something. Presently
Out of this near-chaos an unearthly
Radiance stood like a person in the room,
The memory of the host, perhaps. And all
Fell silent, or stayed at their musings, silent
As before, and no one any longer
Offered words of advice or misgiving, but drank
The silence that had been silence before,
On this scant strip of slag,
Basking in the same light as before,
Inhabiting the same thought:
A shelf of breasts and underwear packaging
Rumored in the dark ages.

These people, you see,
Had to come to appear to thrive
And somewhat later sidestep the destiny
That pretended not to see them.
It was all necessary so that some source,
An origin of the present, might
In the scent of verbena and dreams of
Combat locked in the sky over the mid-ocean
Gradually give less and less of itself

For one to finish examining the elaborate
Mechanical toys of the last century
Or playing warped, scratched 78 records
Of the great coloraturas of the past.
One is always free to sink into history
Up to the waist, and the mountains are
Now so breathtakingly close to the city
That it's like taking a vacation
Just to stay home and look at them.
That's all one can do.

Inhaling the while the extremely cold
Fresh cement smell which you must pass
On your way to school.

For all those with erysipelas
And the wrinkles on the forehead
And the cheeks that come from within, like reverse scars

For all those wearing old clothes
With the dormant look of expectation about them

For the women ironing
And who cut into lengths of white cloth

The glass stopper has been removed
We can breathe! The ocean has been pulled away.

I was over to the dog show the other day and
Noticed a nice-looking girl gazing around
As if puzzled. I went over to her and said:

And in so dying bequeath the manner
Of its being to the sidewalk shrubbery
And so enable it to become itself
Even though that self is only the sometimes-noticed
Backdrop for ourselves and all
We wondered whether we would become,
Pockmarked flecks of polluted matter
Infrequently visible in the hail of ventilated indifference
Or seconds of radiation, our own very special
Thing we had been trying to get our hands
On for so many years.

Honey, it's all Greek to me, I—

(And just to make sure you get
It: *the thought crossed my mind*
That I would do well to take up my studies again,
I seemed to have become less averse to laughter
And less disinclined for certain small pleasures,
And I began quietly to reason with myself
About this matter, as I usually do about others,
So that I regretfully concluded
That I would soon again be the same man as before—)

Meaning: *the same nausea when I heard cheerful talk,*
The same grief, the same deep and prolonged meditation,
And almost the same frenzy and oppression.

Supposing that you are a wall
And can never contribute to nature anything
But the feeling of being alongside it,

"Pardon me, but can't you find the kennel
You wish?
If not, I shall be glad to assist you."

"Oh, thank you!" she replied. "Would you
Mind showing me where they are exhibiting the ocean
greyhounds?"

I came out here originally I
Came to this flat place
On the side away from the sun,
I think my stain must be cauterized.
I have touched no drink
For an elevenmonth, yet my head
Seems stuck in my collar. I have
No friends because I move too rapidly
From place to place, only an assistant.
The time is always false dawn
In Indian Summer. Faded markings on
The floor where I walk could have
Been produced by me, or at best
Some outside agency. I have no reason
To rejoice in my mummy condition, yet
Am fairly happy from day to day
Like a steeple rejoicing in the sun
It is the last to shake hands with.
I wear my weather
With a good-natured air of secrecy,
And have no trouble finding my way home
Once the fun is done. I can sleep.

A certain luxury, and now,
They come to you with the old matter
Of your solidity, that firmness,
That way you have of squaring off
The maps of distant hills, so that nature
Seems farther apart from itself because of you.
Is it this you have done?
And a certain grassy look, the color
Of old semiprecious stones, has to be
What's coming out of you, for the two of you.
And the mechanical reverie is cut up by fits
Of blaring trumpets and alarms, in the night.

Forward then into the yellow villages.
Despite the eerie setbacks
Of our subpolar ambience, *we are*
Living, we are dwelling on a network
Of insane desires handled frugally.
Passport in hand, we arrive in the morning
At the station, the dumb train
Vaults you along into forests of
Broccoli, or tracts of leathery
Tundra, one eye on the digital watch.
The tonal purity grows, and dissipates,
But meanwhile the plateau remains staunch,
It's only the towers that dot it that tend
To look pierced by the sky
Or fade away absentmindedly, altogether.

The naked report arrived vividly
In the night.

I can stand up. The buzzing in the vault
Of the temple disturbs me only insofar
As I consult my pocket watch and replace it
Affably in my breast-pocket. But
There is a time and a light
Which do not approach, which leave me
In the years.

Don't flog it. Remember how
Insane your other undertakings seemed to you,
How hopeless your desires, how tortured
The ambience, or riddled
With the stuff of hazard.
The orgy
Bubbles away, the vapors weep their burthen to the ground.
But in that hotel
The night is ongoing, the rain
Continues. Too much of a philosophy
Is about all it can stand, and we wait
For the men and ducks to go away, and still
Most everything stays with us,
Rooted in thoughtful soil.
The elephant's-foot umbrella stand
That used to be over there, why,
Somebody must have changed it, or the last
Catastrophe fished it up out of the depths
Beyond heaven, or it is here,
For us to see, yet absent for a while.
Or perhaps someone merely heard of it
Or it got written down the wrong way
In a page of an account book that got mailed

Groaning for the latter day brought us
To this place, a trough of silent chatter
Between two notable waves. And we must arrange
These filaments of silence as an elephant trap
Over the grid of city conversations and background doings.
The quietude
Of the future to be built, beside which
Today's valors and sighs must appear
As vanished suburbs beside some eighteenth-century
Metropolis, or stairs rolling down to a sea
Of urgent scrolls and torsades:
A Baltic commonplace riven by tremendous
Hairline fissures as deep as the heavens.
In other words, leave it alone.

That's interesting. In my diary
I have noted down all kinds of exceptional
Things to go with the rest
As one who naps beside a chasm
Swollen with the hellish sound of wind
And torrents, and never chooses
To play back the tape. Waking
Refreshed if not alert, he steps forth
Into the centuries that grew like shadows
Under tall trees while he slept;
The days rub off like scales, the years
Like burrs or briars plucked
Patiently from the sleeve, and never sees
Or hears the havoc wrought by his passing,
Abysses that open up behind
His perilous, beribboned journey, the jalopy

In a letter by mistake. Perhaps the dust,
That emptiness on the outside of air, ate it.
Or in the bin of odd-size and discontinued
Artifacts it holds its own while seen
Only partially because the surrounding
Knobs and hues rob it of a full presence.
Or a photograph was taken, after which
It could be destroyed, and now
The photograph and the negative are lost
Up ahead in one of the strands
Where one shall encounter this and all the
Other deviating forms of momentary life
In a contradiction which shall make its point.

I like to imagine though
That nothing so awkward as the stand ever
Existed. It must have been
The trunk of an old apple tree
And bees hollowed it out to make honey,
Itself now gone, a remnant
Of a memory, a gesture time made
To no one in particular, to itself
Or not even to itself, a tic,
A twinge long invisible now
On the low-pressure area
On the weather map. A tremor
Far removed from the individual man
And his daily wants, a number
To be looked up in a book, or the catalogue number
Of that book, or both,
The number in the book and the catalogue number

Disappearing deep into vales
To re-emerge suddenly on heights, through
The tunnel of a giant sequoia. And always
An old-time mannerliness and courtesy informs
The itinerary, leaving us
Without much to go on.

Once it becomes fatality,
Of course,
The journey is at an end, and it is just beginning—
Innate—
A moody performance.
The critics hated it.
Now one borrows money from his friends,
In double time, the consequences
Blur the motives. The contours of the figures
Are curved and fat. He goes out among the trees,
Sees the lights in the valley far below.
Up here the air is black, ice-cold, of a
Terrifying purity, doubled over somehow.
But your story isn't getting boring,
On the contrary, the slowing-down speeds up the
Afterthought. We are perverse spelling and punctuation.

It could not be confirmed
That the recent violent storms were a part of the pattern
Of civil calamity that had overtaken the outpost.
Perhaps they were fatal but parallel,
Wounds inflicted on a corpse, footnotes
To the desert, the explosion
That a quiet, mediocre career is. We read

In white guano on the brilliant cranberry binding,
Concerns galore
Under both headings, the identical twin numbers.

Ours, actually, is an "age on ages telling,"
Once it has become finality. Afterwards,
It drifts like a stalagmite, advancing
Pea-brained arguments an inch forward.
Of course all this has to go on
Parallel to the hoping, so as to display
The ancestral linkage, and, more importantly, to drown out
Any rumors of competing loyalties.
It is merely a question of avoiding the shadow
And the starched patch of light,
At the same time deferring to no sun,
No shore. No half-naked limit,
And, in the orange light that the sun succeeds nevertheless
In shedding all over this terrestrial ball, to avert
One's gaze no longer and no less time than is intended
By the illuminating party to be your account
Of yourself, here on earth and for all time.

A grand army of fatality succeeding
One after the other like a phylloxera
Never succeeded in erasing intimate
Knowledge of how long that was supposed to be
Despite ferocious efforts from age to age the same
From the minds of those men in which it had been planted
Originally, and who continued to keep up
With the changing time and modes while retaining
With no effort at all,

Through some Haydn quartet movements last night
But this morning my hand and heart are heavy, heavy alack.

The day before yesterday it seemed to me
That my cherished sorrow was about to depart,
And yesterday morning too. And now, fatality
Has overtaken it. The end
Has been quiet, and no one has told the rabbits
And dying bees. Finally some warmth
From the death floated downstream to us,
Saving a few moments of mildness
Among the by-now unmanageably thick grease-crayon
Outline that coagulates like a ball of soot in the air
Watched by hemophiliac princes, like an orange.

And as mushrooms spring up
After great rains have purged the heavens
Of their terrible delight, so the weight of event
And counterevent conspired to shift the focus
Of the scenery away from the action:
It was always wartime Britain, or some other place
Dictated by the circumstances, never
The road leading over the hill
To yet another home. Rudeness, shabbiness—
We could have put up with more than a little
Of these in the hope of getting some bed-rest,
But a measured calm, maddening in
Its insularity, always prevailed at the window,
Priming the hour with anguish, and yet
It was never any later, there was never anything
More to do, everybody kept telling you

As though all were elegy and toccata
(Which happens to be the case),
The guidelines. Once given
They can be forgotten in the sad joy of life,
Reverence for which is almost incumbent
On each contestant, and no one, including them,
Will ever be wider for it. Yet
Thereby hangs a tale, of starving musicians,
Strolling players, grasshopper and the ant
Whose contemptible fireside contrasts so untellingly
With the barren outdoors. Just to play an instrument,
It seems, is to have to come round one
Day to the impossibility of making a living on it,
To being forced to prostitute oneself, innocently,
For the greater pleasure which is as the damage
Succeeding on the small first pleasure.
And there's no way out, unless
The sound of harps is sufficient distraction
Against the thunder of the "fray" for which
Gog and Magog are said to be continually preparing,
Or loss of memory (which cannot, by definition,
Take place) render one oblivious to the traffic
And all it implies. That loss of memory
Which is itself a music,
A kind of music.
And meanwhile, growing older like leaves that lean back
Against the trees, is an accomplishment
Without comfort.

Back home from the beauty contest
And its attendant squalors, she doesn't feel

To relax until you were ready to scream,
And now this patient night has infused,
In whose folds only one soul is awake, in the whole wide
    world.

Feeling no need to look at the world through
    rose-colored glasses,
To get by on "cuteness,"
To create large new forms and people them with space,
You thwart any directions, right or wrong.
The *séduction de l'âme* will not take place.
The long rains in November, November
Of long rains, silent woods,
Open like a compass to receive the anomaly,
Press it back into the damp earth,
The shadow of a whisper on someone's lips.

You can neither define
Nor erase it, and, seen by torchlight,
Being cloaked with the shrill
Savage drapery of non-being, it
Stands out in the firelight.
It is more than anything was meant to be.
Yet somehow mournful, as though
The three-dimensional effect had been achieved
At the cost of a crisp vagueness
That raised one twig slightly higher than the
Morass of leafless branches that supported it,
And now, eager, fatigued, it had sunk back
Below the generally satisfying
Contours of the rest. It had eaten

Like much. The world
Is vaguer and less pejorative, a time
Of stressful headache but also
Of architectonic inklings and inspiration:
Agony for a day, and then the refreshing dream
Bubbles up like an artesian well in all its
Wealth of accurately observed detail,
Its truth of being, on the surface
But striking long, pointed roots into the dull earth
Behind the mask. Yet like a pain
That went away, its immanence
Is very much an ongoing thing, its present
Departed in the greater interest of the whole.
A coronet of dark red jewels
Like winter berries was slowly lowered
Onto the snow-white curls, and the dream became
A person, a beautiful princess unable to stand
Or sit. And the older guests remembered
How none of it had been predicted, though the mystery
    word,
"Magic," had been imagined
Many years before. How
Do we live from the beginning of the tale
To its inevitable, momentary end, where all
Its pocket's treasures are summarily emptied
On the mirroring tabletop? And wait
For someone to whisper the word that restores them
To their velvet hummock, sets all right again?

Only the cartoon animals know
How hard it was to get inside the frame, and then

The food you gave it, and kept to itself
Mainly, in a corner of the pen.
You never spoke to it except in the kindest
Tones, and it replied sadly,
If somewhat politely, and how much, now
You wish you had kept a record of those exchanges!
One thing is sure: nothing
Can replace it; as fatally
As it was given to you, so now
It has been removed from you, for your comfort,
And nothing stands in its place.

It is not a question of emptiness, only
Of a place the others never seem to venture,
A sunken Parnassus.
There is a slight change, a chance rather
Of its coming to life at the reunion,
Amid the automatic greetings, summonses
From a brazen tongue:

"And so you thought this
Was where he brought you, the
Updated silhouette, late sunlight
Developed on the tallest slope, to the assignation
Rumored so often, to a corral
Shaped like a snowflake, and love
Blurring each of the points. Yet you
Stand fast and cannot see
Where it is leading. And the seducer remains at home."

To make a noise, or eventually to place
An inky paw-print on the wide, blinding white
Damask desert as the company was leaving
In twos and threes. Someone
Projects a shriek of recognition far up, into the civilized
But dim world of the farthest chandelier.
A commercial airliner streaked by. Once again
The prize will not be awarded.
The distant plains match up with
The pictures of them on these transparent walls,
And that is all. No children
To relieve the tensions of the adult business,
No new funny animals, only the vocal abstractions
Of the solemn, imaginary world of transportation
And commerce. No one
Laughs at the brilliant errors any more.

Yet we who came to know them,
Castaways of middle life, somehow
Grew aware through the layers of numbing comfort,
The eiderdown of materialism and space, how much
    meaning
Was there languishing at the roots, and how
To take some of it home before it melts (as all
Will, dreams and mica-sparkling sidewalks, clouds
And office buildings, the conversation
And the trance, until
A day when they can do no more, and the mass
Of the scenery wanders partially
Over the defunct terrain of broken fences
And windows stuffed with rags) while the ballad

Still rings in the seller's ear.

In the beginning of speech the question
Of frontiers is taken up again.
And the trees and buildings are porous
And the dome of heaven.

The talk leads nowhere but is
Inside its space.

It is contracting, it is observed . . .
Breath we wanted, to build and lie down
In slumber at night, under the tattered shade
Of the trees, open to the rain, rustling of night.
And the wet, doggy smell,
The pealing of church bells interspersed with thunder
And lightning, the distress
And tiny triumphs of the field.
Everything is a shaft
Sunk far too deep into the body, opening landscapes,
New people, mingling in new conversations,
Yet distant, as the back of one's head is distant.
It all seems like 2½ years ago
To the impatient sun trapped in the attic
When all it wants is to be able to write about mathematics
    and the word,
For although a few wind-chime notes filter down
From heaven in the small hours, one cannot help
But note the frequent fanfare of hoofbeats
In the wet, empty street.
No one said it would turn out this way

But of course, no one knew, and now most of them
Are dead.

           One, however, still looms,
Billboard-size in the picaresque
Night sky of eleven years ago. And whose
Hand is it, placed comically against your throat,
Emerging from a checkered cuff? Because a long time ago
You were promised safe-conduct
From a brief, mild agony
To these not-uninteresting pangs of birth
And so, and so, a landscape always seen through black lace
Became this institution
For you, inflected, as we shall see,
From time to time by discreet nautical allusions
And shreds of decor, to amount
To these handfuls and no other: a reminder
To keep it soft and straight forever as long
As no other pick up your ringing phone.
Play it on any instrument. It is in whack
And ready to do your bidding, though sunk
In the rat-infested heap of rose embers
Of the terminating day. A keepsake.

This has been a remarkable afternoon:
The sky turned pitch-black at some point though there
Was still enough light to see things by.
Everything looked very festive and elegant
Against the inky backdrop. But who cares?
Isn't it normal for things to happen this way
During the Silver Age, which ours is?
Motifs like the presentation of the Silver Rose

Yet whereto, with damaged wing
Assay th'empyrean? Scalloped horizon
Of Cloud-Cuckoo-Land? O land
Of recently boiling water, witches'
Misgivings, ships
Pulling away from piers,
Already slipping deep into the norm
Of blue worsted seas? Yet that is just what I did.

There are always those who think you ought to
Turn back from dull autumn sunsets like whey in the breeze
  that escorts
Us up inclined planes whose appearance, dull too
At first, is experienced
As if bathed in magic, when its density,
"A flash of lightning, seen in passing and very faintly,"
Stuns the apprehending faculties
With the perfection of its desire
Like the scream of the rising moon.
It is best to abide with minstrels, then,
To play at least one game
Seriously. The old-timers will
Let you take over the old lease.
One of them will be in you.

If there were concerts on the water there
We could turn back. Tar floated upriver
In the teeth of the gulls' outlandish manifestations;
The banks pocked with flowers whose names
I used to know,
Before poetic license took over and abolished everything.
People shade their eyes and wave
From the strand: to us or someone behind us?
Just as everything seemed about to go wrong
The music began; later on, the missing
Refreshments would be found and served,
The road turn caramel just as the first stars
Were putting in a timid appearance, like snowdrops.
And somehow you found the strength

Abound, and no one really pays much attention
To anything at all. People
Are either too stunned or too engrossed
In their own petty pursuits to bother with
What is happening all around them, even
When that turns out to be extremely interesting
As is now so often the case.
You will see them buying tickets
To this or that opera, but how many times
Will they tell you whether they enjoyed it
Or anything? Sometimes
I think we are being punished for the overabundance
Of things to enjoy and appreciate that we have,
By being rendered less sensitive to them.
Just one minute of contemporary existence
Has so much to offer, but who
Can evaluate it, formulate
The appropriate apothegm, show us
In a few well-chosen words of wisdom
Exactly what is taking place all about us?
Not critics, certainly, though that is precisely
What they are supposed to be doing, yet how
Often have you read any criticism
Of our society and all the people and things in it
That really makes sense, to us as human beings?
I don't mean that a lot that is clever and intelligent
Doesn't get written, both by critics
And poets and men-of-letters in general
But exactly whom are you aware of
Who can describe the exact feel
And slant of a field in such a way as to

To be carried irresistibly away from all this.

But in the scrapbooks and postcard albums
Of the land, you are remembered,
Although you do not figure there,
And because a train once passed near where
You spent a night, a tall, translucent
Monument like a spike has been erected to your memory,
Only do not go there. One can live
In the land like a spy without ever
Trespassing on the mortal, forgotten frontier.
In the psalms of the invisible chorus
There is a germ of you that lives like a coal
Amid the hostile indifference of the land
That merely forgets you. Your hand
Is at the heart of its weavings and nestlings.
You are its guarantee.

At that moment, fatality
Or some woman resembling her, angel,
Goddess, whatever: "the Beautiful Lady"
Arrives to announce the Brass Age—
"You are being asked to believe
No more in the subtle possibilities of silver,
Which, like the tintinnabulation of an ethereal
Silver chime, marking an unknown hour
From a remote, dismal room, no longer
Promises harvests, only the translucent melancholy
Of the skies which follow in their wake,
Pale, greenish blue, with magnificent
Clouds like overloaded schooners, that dip

Make you wish you were in it, or better yet
To make you realize that you actually are in it
For better or for worse, with no
Conceivable way of getting out?
That is what
Great poets of the past have done, and a few
Great critics as well. But today
Nobody cares or stands for anything,
Not even the handful of poets one admires, though
You don't see them quitting the poetry business,
Far from it. It behooves
Our critics to make the poets more aware of
What they're doing, so that poets in turn
Can stand back from their work and be enchanted by it
And in this way make room for the general public
To crowd around and be enchanted by it too,
And then, hopefully, make some sense of their lives,
Bring order back into the disorderly house
Of their drab existences. If only
They could see a little better what was going on
Then this desirable effect might occur,
But today's artists and writers won't have it,
That is they don't see it that way.
They do see a certain way, and that way
Is interesting to them, but
Doesn't help your average baker or cheerleader
To see precisely the same way, which
Is the only thing that could rescue them
From the desperate, tangled muddle of their
Frustrated, unsatisfactory living. Seeing things
In approximately the same way as the writer or artist

To rise again, higher, and seem
Endlessly on the move, until they round—
What? Is there some cape, some destination,
Some port of debarkation in all this?
There is only the slow but febrile motion
Of sky and cloud, a toast, a promise,
A new diary, until one gets too close
And becomes oneself part of the meaningless
Rolling and lurching, so hard to read
Or hear, and never closer
To the end or to the beginning: the mimesis
Of death, without the finality—is
There anything in this for you?
Sad, browning flowers, tokens
Of the wind's remembering you, damp, rotting
Nostalgia under a head of twigs or at the end
Of some log spangled with brand-new, ice-green lichens,
Dead pine-needles, worthy
Objects of contemplation if you wish, but there is
Less comfort but more interest in the drab
Clear moment that enshrines us
Now, in this place. No one
Could mistake this for morning, or afternoon,
Or the specious perfection of twilight, yet
It is within us, and the substance
Of your latest interventions. Therefore, begone!"

The voice
Straddled the stone canyon like vapors.
In the distance one could see oneself, drawn
On the air like one of Millet's "Gleaners," extracting

Doesn't help either, in fact, if anything, it makes things
*   worse*
Because then the other person thinks he
Or she has found out whatever it is that makes
Art interesting to them, the reason
For those diamond tears on the scarlet
Velvet of the banquette at the opera,
And goes on a rampage, featuring his or her emotions
As the banners with a strange device of a new revolution
Of the senses, but it's doomed
To end in failure, unless that person happens to be
Exactly the same person as the artist who is doing
All this to them, which of course is impossible,
Impossible at any rate in a Silver Age
Wherein a multitude of glittering, interesting
Things and people attack one
Like a blizzard at every street crossing
Yet remain unseen, unknown and undeveloped
In the electrical climate of sensitivities that ask
Only for self-gratification,
Not for outside or part-time help
In assimilating and enjoying whatever it is.
Therefore a new school of criticism must be developed.
First of all, the new
Criticism should take into account that it is we
Who made it, and therefore
Not be too eager to criticize us: we
Could do that for ourselves, and have done so.
Nor
Should it take itself as a fitting subject
For critical analysis, since it knows

This or that from the vulgar stubble, with the roistering
Of harvesters long extinct, dead for the ear, and in the
    middle
Distance, one's new approximation of oneself:
A seated figure, neither imperious nor querulous,
No longer invoking the riddle of the skies, of distance,
Nor yet content with the propinquity
Of strangers and admirers, all rapt,
In attitudes of fascination at your feet, waiting
For the story to begin.

All right. Let's see—
How about "The outlook wasn't brilliant
For the Mudville nine that day"? No,
That kind of stuff is too old-hat. Today
More than ever readers are looking for
Something upbeat, to sweep them off their feet.
Something candid but also sophisticated
With an unusual slant. A class act
That doesn't *look* like a class act
Is more like . . .

It goes without saying
That I enjoy
You as you are,
The pleasant taste of you.
You are with me as the seasons
Circle with us around the sun
That dates back to the seventeenth century,
We circling with them,
United with ourselves and directly linked

Itself only through us, and us
Only through being part of ourselves, the bark
Of the tree of our intellect. What then
Shall it criticize, in order to dispel
The quaint illusions that have been deluding us,
The pictures, the trouvailles, the sallies
Swallowed up in the howl? Whose subjects
Are these? Yet all
Is by definition subject matter for the new
Criticism, which is us: to inflect
It is to count our own ribs, as though Narcissus
Were born blind, and still daily
Haunts the mantled pool, and does not know why.

It's sad the way they feel about it—
Poetry—
As though it could synchronize our lives
With our feelings about ourselves,
And form a bridge between them and "life"
As we come to think about it.
No one has ever really done a good piece
On all the things a woman carries inside her pocketbook,
For instance, and there are other ways
Of looking out over wide things.
And yet the sadness is already built into
The description. Who can begin
To describe without feeling it?
So many points of view, so many details
That are probably significant. And when
We have finished writing our novel or
Critical essay, what it does say, no matter

To them, changing as they change,
Only their changes are always the same, and we,
We are always a little different with each change.
But in the end our changes make us into something,
Bend us into some shape maybe
No one we would recognize,
And it is ours, anyway, beyond understanding
Or even beyond our perception:
We may never perceive the thing we have become.
But that's all right—we have to be it
Even as we are ourselves. Anyway,
That's the way I like you and the way
Things are going to be increasingly,
With the seasons a mirror of our indeterminate
Activities, so that they do end
In burgeoning leaves and buds and then
In bare twigs against a Pater-painted
Sky of gray, expecting snow . . .
How can we know ourselves through
These excrescences of time that take
Their cues elsewhere? Whom
Should I refer you to, if I am not
To be of you? But you
Will continue in your own way, will finish
Your novel, and have a life
Full of happy, active surprises, curious
Twists and developments of character:
A charm is fixed above you
And everything you do, but you
Must never make too much of it, nor
Take it for granted, either. Anyway, as

How good it is, it merely mocks the idea
Of a whole comprised by all those now mostly invisible
Ideas, ghosts
Of things and reasons for them,
So that it takes over, seizes the glitter
And luminosity of what ought to have been our
Creative writing, even though it is dead
Or was never called to life, and could not be
Anything living, like what we managed
Somehow to get down on the page.
And the afternoon backs off,
Won't have anything to do with all of this.

Yet the writing that doesn't offend us
(Keats' "grasshopper" sonnet for example)
Soothes and flatters the easier, less excitable
Parts of our brain in such a way as to set up a
Living, vibrant turntable of events,
A few selected ones, that nonetheless have
Their own veracity and their own way of talking
Directly into us without any effort so
That we can ignore what isn't there—
The death patterns, swirling ideas like
Autumn leaves in the teeth of an insane gale,
And can end up really reminding us
How big and forceful some of our ideas can be—
Not giants or titans, but strong, firm
Human beings with a good sense of humor
And a grasp of a certain level of reality that
Is going to be enough—will have to be,
And so lead us gradually back to words

I said, I like you this way, understood
If under-appreciated, and finally
My features come to rest, locked
In the gold-filled chain of your expressions,
The one I was always setting out to be—
Remember? And now it is so.

Yet—whether it wasn't all just a little,
Well, silly, or whether on the other hand this
Wasn't a welcome sign of something
Human at last, like a bird
After you've been sailing on and on for days:
How could we tell
The serene and majestic side of nature
From the other one, the mocking and swearing
And smoke billowing out of the ground?
Because they are so closely and explicitly
Intertwined that good
Oftentimes seems merely the necessary
Attractive side of evil, which in turn
Can be viewed as the less appealing but more
Human side of good, something at least
Which can be appreciated?
But poetry is making things in the past;
The past tense transcends and excuses these
Grimy arguments which fog over as soon as
You begin to contemplate them. Poetry
Has already happened. And the agony
Of looking steadily at something isn't
Really there at all, it's something you
Once read about; its narrative thrust

With names we had forgotten, old friends from
Childhood, and then everything
Is forgiven at last, and we
Can sit and talk quietly with them for hours,
Words ourselves, so that when sleep comes
No one is to blame, and no reproach
Can finally be uttered as the lamp
Is trimmed. The tales
Live now, and we live as part of them,
Caring for them and for ourselves, warm at last.

All life
Is as a tale told to one in a dream
In tones never totally audible
Or understandable, and one wakes
Wishing to hear more, asking
For more, but one wakes to death, alas,
Yet one never
Pays any heed to that, the tale
Is still so magnificent in the telling
That it towers far above life, like some magnificent
Cathedral spire, far above the life
Pullulating around it (what
Does it care for that, after all?) and not
Even aiming at the heavens far above it
Yet seemingly nearer, just because so
Vague and pointless: the spire
Outdistances these, and the story
With its telling, which is like gothic
Architecture seen from a great distance,
Booms on in such a way

Carries it far beyond what it thought it was
All het up about; its charm, no longer
A diversionary tactic, is something like
Grace, in the long run, which is what poetry is.
Musing on these things he turned off the
Great high street which is like a too-busy
Harbor full of boats knocking against each
Other, a blatantly cacophonous if stirring
Symphony, with all its most
Staggeringly beautiful aspects jammed against
The lowest motives and inspirations that ever
Infected the human spirit, into a
Small courtyard continued by an alley as
Though a sudden hush or drop in the temperature
Suddenly fell across him, like steep
Building-shadows, and he wondered
What it had all been leading up to. Up there
Wisps of smoke raced away from grimy
Chimney pots as though pursued by demons;
Down here all was yellowing silence and
Melancholy though not without a secret
Feeling of satisfaction at having escaped
The rat race, if only for a time, to plunge
Into profitless meditations, as threadbare
As the old mohair coat he had worn from
Earliest times, and which no one
Had ever seen him doff, no matter
What the prevailing meteorological conditions were.
These were now the fabric
Of his existence, and fabric was precisely
What he felt that existence to be: something old

As to make us forget the prodigious
Distance of the waking from the
Thing that was going on, in the novel
We had been overhearing, all that time.
Not that writing can transcend life,
Any more than the act of writing can
Outdistance the imagination it feeds on and
Imitates in its ductility, its swift
Garrulity, jumping from line to line,
From page to page: it is both
Too remote and too near to transcend it,
It is it, probably, and this is what
We have awakened only to hear: maybe just
A long list of complaints or someone's
Half-formed notions of what they thought
About something, too greedy
Even to feed on itself, and therefore
Lost in the muck
Of sleep and all that is forever outside,
Condemned to be told, and never
To hear of itself.

Sometimes a pleasant, dimpling
Stream will seem to flow so slowly all of a
Sudden that one wonders if it was this
Rather than the other that one was supposed to read.
In the charmèd air one
Imagines one hears waltzes, ländler, and écossaises
And concludes that it is literature
That is doing it, and that therefore
It must do it all the time. It works out too well,

And useful, useful and useless at the same time.

I was waiting for a taxi.
It seemed there were fewer
Of us now, and suddenly a
Whole lot fewer. I was afraid
I might be the only one.
Then I spotted a young man
With a guitar over his leg
And next to him, a young girl
Seated on the pavement, sitting
Merely. Not even
Lost in thought she seemed, but
Accepting the waiting for it
Or whatever else might be in the channel
Of time we were being ferried across.
Her face was totally devoid of expression
Yet wore a somehow kind look, so I was glad
Of it in the deepening fever of the day.
No sign
Did she make of interest to her companion
Who ever and anon did searchingly
Regard her face, as though to ascertain
That the signs he wished to read there
Were indeed not there, that there was nothing
In her aspect to cause him to change
And from time to time
Would stare at his guitar, as though
Rapt in concentration of what it would be like
To play something on it, yet
No stealthy movement of his hand

The ending is too happy
For it to be life, and therefore it must
Be the product of some deluded poet's brain: life
Could never be this satisfactory, nor indulge
That truly human passion to be all alone.

And I too am concerned that it
Be this way for you. That you
Get something out of it too.
Otherwise the night has no end.

Otherwise the weeping messiah
Who comforts us on those nights
When truth has flown out the window
Would never place an asterisk
On your heart. Your whole life
Would be like walking through a field
Of tall grasses, in time with the wind
As it blows. And in old age
There will have been no jump to the barefaced
Old man you then are, only a nudge
And promise of more suppers: some things I have to do.

How is it that you get from this place
To that one only a little distance away
Without anybody's seeing you do it?
The trip to the basement
Performed unseen, unknown . . .
Uncle Fred and his cigars
All my old Mildred Bailey records
And a highly intelligent kangaroo

Was e'er discerned, no fandango or urgent
Serenade compelled his trusting back
To arch in expectation of an air
Which might have refreshed us all, given
The gloom of that moment, made us think
Of past scenes of cheerfulness, and remember
That they could easily happen again, unless
The mechanism had jammed, and we
Were to be tenants forever of a time
With little to hold the interest, and no
Promise of relief in movement.

And afterwards it was as though decay
Or senility of time had set in.
The scene changed, of course, and nothing
Was, again, as once it had been.
And therefore I do not see how I
Shall ever be able to acquire again
My old love of study, for it seems to me
That even when this infirmity of time
Has passed, the knowledge
Will always remain with me that there is one
Thing more delightful than study, and that once
I experienced it. And though it was not joy
But rather something more like the concept of joy,
I was able to experience it like a fruit
One peels, then eats. It's no secret
That I have learned the things that are
Truly impossible, and left alone much
That might have been of profit, and use.
One destroys so much merely by pausing

Riding with me, all of us in the back seat
In our old Hudson.

It doesn't explain much—
Rituals don't—
But as frantic as the commotion in nature
Now is, the grand impermanence
Of this storm, impatience
Of the calm skies to start again,
The house stays much the same.
One day a little bit of rust
At the eaves, a bit of tape removed
And its story will have been elsewhere,
Soon removed, like a porch, and the head
Must again sneeze out an idea of flowers.
That music, the same old one, will be born again.

So much for the resident way
Of adding up the drawbacks and the satisfactions
If any are to be found, and
I salute you so as you enjoy
The mellow fecund death of that past.
Ah'm impressed. And should we
Never get together, the deal stands.
We want it for them and we and us
More than ever now that it has dwindled
To a sticky, unsightly root. But now
The present has dried out in front of the fire
And we must resume the flight again.

Someone who likes you first

To get one's bearings, and afterwards
The scent is lost. To use it
I must forget the clouds and turn to my book,
Whose shifting characters, like desert sand
Betray my own fatigue, and loss
Of time, that ever, with nervous, accurate fingers
Cross-hatches the shade in the corner
Of the piazza where I stand, and leave
The lighted areas scarcely perforated, almost
Pristine. Lovers in parked cars
Undulated like the sensibility that refrigerates
Me at those times: and who
Could pick up the pieces, over and over?

Yes, it was a fine gift that you sent
Me, your book, wherein I could read
The very syllables of your soul, as dark-arched
And true as any word
You ever grunted, and whose truant
Punctuation resumed again the thread
Of what is outside, outdoors, and brought
It all ingeniously around to the beginning again
As a fountain swipes and never misses
The basin's fluted edge. But how in
Heck can I get it operating again? Only
Yesterday it was in perfect working order
And now the thing has broken down again.
Autumn rains rust it. And their motion
Attacks my credulity also, and all seems lost.
Yet fences were not ever built to last:
A year or two and all is blown away

Comes along. The act is open
And a nation of stargazers begins
To unwrap the fever of forgetting, the while
You sidle next to each other and never
Afterward shall it be a question of these blooms
In that time, of speech heard
In that apartment. Nowhere that the light comes
Can you and he argue the subtle hegemony
Of guilt that loops you together
In the continual crisis of a rood-screen
Pierced here and there with old commercials
Shimmering and shining in the sun.
You are cast down into the lowest place
In the universe, and you both love it.
All this time larger and I may say graver
Destinies were being unfurled on the political front
And in the marketplace, important issues
That you are unable and unwilling to understand,
Though you know you ignore them at your peril,
That any schoolchild can recite them now.
Yet somehow it doesn't bode well that
In your sophistication you choose to disregard
What is so heavy with potential tragic consequences
Hanging above you like a storm cloud
And cannot know otherwise, even by diving
Into the shallow stream of your innocence
And wish not to hear news of
What brings the world together and sets fire to it.
It wasn't innocence even then, but a desire to
Keep the severe sparkle of childhood for
The sudden moments of maturity that come

And no trace can be found.

                    As a last blessing
Bestow this piece of shrewd, regular knowledge
On me who hungers so much for something
To calm his appetite, not food necessarily—
The pattern behind the iris that lights up
Your almost benevolent eyelash: turn
All this anxious scrutiny into some positive
Chunk to counteract the freedom
Of too much speculation. Tell me
What is on your mind, and do not explain it away.

"The egrets are beginning their annual migration.
From the banks of the Hag River a desolate
Convoy issues, like a directional pointing hand.
There is a limit to what the wilderness
Can accomplish on its own, and meanwhile,
Back in civilization, you don't seem to be
Doing too well either: those flying
Bits of newspaper and plastic bags scarce
Bode better for him who sits and picks at
The secret, when suddenly
The meaning knocks him down, a light bulb
Appears in a balloon above his head: it had nothing
To do with what the others were thinking, what
Energies they poured into the mould of their
Collective statement. It was only
As a refugee from all this that living
Were possible if at all, but it cast no shadow,
No reflection in the mirror, and was nervous
And waifed, so strong was the shuttle

Surprisingly in the night, dazzling
By the very singleness of their passage
Like white blossoming trees glimpsed
In the May night, before the tempests of summer
Put an end to all dreams of sailing and hoped-for
Good weather and luck, before the frosts come
Like magic garments. And so
I say unto you: beware the right margin
Which is unjustified; the left
Is justified and can take care of itself
But what is in between expands and flaps
The end sometimes past the point
Of conscious inquiry, noodling in the near
Infinite, off-limits. Therefore
All your story should be phrased so that
Tinkers and journeymen may inspect it
And find it all in place, and pass on
Or suddenly on a night of profound sleep
The thudding of a moth's body will awaken you
And drag you with it vers la flamme,
Kicking and screaming. And then
What might have been written down is seen
To have been said, and heard, and silence
Has flowed around the place again and covered it.

"*The morning cometh, and also the night.*"
I'll dampen you
As I celebrate you, but first
I'll turn your feet over
And enjoy you with this ever slenderer
Aspen climate, as one in the know would do.

Of accurate presentiment plying directly
Between it and the discarded past. Playing
A game is the only way to see it through, and have it
Finally integral, but the matter is that
This is somewhere else: its rails
Run deep into the leafy wilderness, sink
And disappear under moss and slime
Long before the end is reached. It's a crime,
And meanwhile your velvet portrait presides,
Benevolent as Queen Anne, over the scene
Below, and at no point
Do reality and your joyous truth coincide."

So sang one who was in prison, and the erosion
Process duly left its mark
On the wall:
Only a wan, tainted shadow leaned
Down from the place where it had been.
The eroding goes on constantly in the brain
Where its music is softest, a lullaby
On the edge of a precipice where the whole movement
Of the night can be seen:
How it begins, undresses, and disappears
In hollows before the level is seen to rise.
And then we are in a full, static music,
Violent and spongy as bronze, but
There is no need, no chance to examine
The accidents of the surface that stretches away
Forever, toward the ultramarine gates
Of the horizon of this tidal basin, and beyond,
Pouring silently into the vast concern

I'll mouth expressions of yours
And replay your tricycle in the formal walks
And garden beds. Some very pretty views
Can be ascertained now. I'll not
Put a glove on so you may see the snake
With the cobalt eyes, and bring you offerings
Of olives, bananas, guavas, Japanese persimmons.
   Furthermore,
I will await you in indolence, so that
The view of the sea will move in slowly
And become the walls of this room.
But it was on this day that
I wanted to do something,
Commemorate something,
Not "never" or that day coming up.
So I offer you everything
You may ever want, not
Knowing how I'll pay the bills, just
Keeping to the memory of it like larkspur
Or a bird's head I once saw in a forest at dusk.
Lots of them are coming to prepare you
For this, and if I can't have you
I'll figure out some way out of this
Until the hour tolls its distinction
Amid great bravery and truth
Where men are seen running in and around from all over
And the rendition of great sonatas
May then be seen to give back some fitful,
Momentary spark of "the" truth
As cedars blacken against the fence and the sky
Just before slipping through the buttonhole of truth—

Of heaven, in which the greatest explanation
Is but a drop in the bucket of eternity;
Mon rêve.
But why, in that case,
Whispered the petitioner, pushing her
Magenta lips close to the thick wire mesh
That separated them, rubbing
Her gloved hand athwart it as though
Devoured now by curiosity, can God
Let the eroding happen at all, since it is all,
As you say, horizontal, without
Beginning or end, and seamless
At the horizon where it bends
Into a past which has already begun? In
Truth, then, if we are particles of anything
They must belong to our conception
Of our destiny, and be as complete as that.

It's like we were children again: the bicycle
Sighs and the stars pecking at the sky
Are unconstrained in spite of the distance:
The blanket buries us in a joyous tumult
Of indifference when night is
Blackest
So that we grow up again as we were taught to do
Before that. With the increase of joy
The sorrow is precipitated out, and life takes on
An uncanny resemblance to the photograph of me
That everybody said was terrible, only now it is real
And cannot be photographed.
It was nice of you to love me

The commonplace, casual occurrence.
An honest killer would have caught you
And told you that way, and gone away.
But the basin of remorse is so vast
No drop ever increases it, and telling
Only makes it reverberate
Inward upon itself, toward the center that is not there.
And whether you search for nightingales
Or distress signals on the earth's clay lid, all
Is much the same: your face at morning
And your blue-plaid face at evening with no
Expression are nevertheless the same
Until the code is ventilated, and we who have
Come down with you, to the same root or comma,
Are new now, but with no difference.

He would cook up these goulashes
Make everything shipshape
And then disappear, like Hamlet, in a blizzard
Of speculation that comes to occupy
The forefront for a time, until
Nothing but the forefront exists, like a forehead
Of the times, speechless, drunk, imagined
In all its five shapes, and never in one state
Of repose, though always disclosed
And disclosing, keeping itself like a chance
In the dark, living wholly in a dream
Sweet reality discovers.

I wander through each dirty street
Knowing how painted rooms are bonny,

But I must be thinking about getting back
Over the mountain
That divides day from night:
Visions more and more restless
All now sunk in black of Egypt.

The enduring obloquy of a gaze struck
The new year, cracking it open
At the point where people and animals, each busy
With his own thoughts, wandered away
In unnamed directions. If there is a fire,
I thought, why single out the glares
Impaling those least near it
In such a way as to reflect them back
On its solid edifice? But here
In a tissue of starlight, each is alone and valid.
You can stand up to breathe
And the garment falling around you is history,
Someone's, anyway, some perfectly accessible,
Reasonable assessment of the recent past, which
With its pattern dips into the shadow of the folds
To re-emerge and be striking on the crest
Of them somewhere, and thus serves
Twice over, as plan and decoration,
A garden plunged in sun seen through a fixed lattice
Of regrets and doubts, pinned there
For a variety of good reasons, alive, stupid
As a sail stunned in a vast haze,

Perfect for you. And you rise
Imperfect and beautiful as a second, a continent

Remembering feather beds are soft, and Jack,
Eating rotten cheese. As the babble
Of apes in an orchard are the slogans
That solicit us like pennants in the sky:
Fools rush into my head, and so I write.

I'll wipe away all trivial fond records
From the interstices of my desirings
And imaginings, and find the whiteness
That was there. Already the colors of sleep
Are fading, a blankness
Is taking shape, and its magnificent outline
Washes true like the sound of a French horn,
And then somehow, sqwunched or
Scrunched down in the corner, in the folds
It collects itself, again, and all the differences
Are differences among rainbows, or adhesions
In the dance, that dissolve and strengthen
As it reaches its pitch. Again, ambition is seen
As no idle thing. Reading the papers
We are inflamed to emulate it, even as
There seems nothing wrong with it, and finally
Vote for it. Impetuously
We travel on, life seems full of promise,
And ambition is so recent as to be almost
Stronger than living, and makes its own
Definitions and pays for them. Surely
Life is meant to be this way, solemn
And joyful as an autumn wood rent by the hunters'
Horns and their dogs, unmixed with pleasure,
Turned inside out, violating

Whose near coast alone can be seen, but
Which makes up for that in the strength of the confusion
Building behind it, and is at rest.

And I'll tell you why:
The elaborate indifference of some people, of some person
Far out on the curve
Is always rescued by another person
And this will be some forgotten day three years ago
At today's prices. The tensions, overlaid,
Superimposed, produce an effect of "character"
And quizzical harmony, like the outdoors.

But on death's dark river,
On the demon's charcoal-colored heaths
Where the luscious light never falls, but fluffy
Cinders are falling everywhere, the persons
Gesture hurriedly at each other from a distance.
Surely this is no time to play dumb, or dead, but
A directive has not been issued.
At the plant they know no more about it than you do
Here, and in the dump behind
They are singing of something else, trilling surely
But no one any longer can make any sense of it.
It is as though you had paid the bills
But the sun keeps writhing: "For this
I gave apples unto the tawny couch-grass, kept ledgers
In my time, as you do in yours?
That a badger with a trumpet on a far tussock
May rake in the calls, and none of it
Ever gets distributed to the poor, which I had stipulated

The very name of intimacy, but assured
Of an easy victory. Time was when it seemed
Too rich, too filling, but now the lean
Bones of the November wind are seen as dainty,
And just sufficient,
Emblems of the famished year.

O sun, God's creation,
Shine hot for one hour, confounding my enemies
Or else make them like me. I want to write
Poems that are as inexact as mathematics. I have been
Sitting making mudpies, in the sparkling sunlight,
And the difficulty of giving them away
Doesn't matter so long as I want you
To enjoy them. Enjoy these! You are busy, I know,
But could find time for this. Some day
People will remember them—this always happens—
And you'll be caught with your pants down.
Besides, how many streams can you rake
With your copper rake, without counting;
How much pouring fog chase away, larks
And ploughmen delight? In the occupied countries
You are raised to the statute of a god, no one
Questions your work, its validity, all
Are eager only to support it, to give of themselves
So as to push your crowning effort over the top:
Never
Had any such a plebiscite, but you must earn it
Even so, prepare, purify yourself to be worthy of it
Although no one will notice. Then, when you
Are setting, in a blaze of glory, you'll find

As being part of the deal? And who are we poor workers?
Not much surely, but we were
Just getting over the shock of dispossession
When this happened, and now this on top of it.
Who is any the wiser? What are we to make of
What now appears to be our lot, though we did nothing
To deserve it? Our efforts were in some way
Directed at a greater good, though we never forgot
Our own interests, as long as they harmed no one.
And now we are cast out like a stone. Surely
The sun knows something I do not know
Although I am the sun."
                                And slowly
The results are brought in, and are found disappointing
As broken blue birds'-eggs in a nest among rushes
And we fall away like fish from the Grand Banks
Into the inky, tepid depths beyond. It is said
That this is our development, but no one believes
It is, but no one has any authority to proceed further.
And we keep chewing on darkness like a rind
For what comfort it can give in the crevices
Between us, like those between your eyes
When you speak sideways to me, and I cannot
Hear you, though farther out there are those
Who hear you and are encouraged, and their effort
Brightens on the side of the mountain.

"I haven't seen him since I've been here"—and I,
All liking and no indifference, transfixed
By the macaronic, like a florist, weary and slippy-eyed,
Athwart blooms, compose, out of what the day provides,

You have already written about this, about all
That's already happened, and everything that could be
In the future, and won't mind
About disappearing behind yon crag
Which already is grown silent, erect
With waiting, tense and eager as a bridegroom
For you to fall alongside its spine:

"The protector
  Came from the tussock, the son rose up from the bottom."

I have heard that in spring the mountains change
And seldom pay any mind to the sun (who continues,
Nonetheless, to do good deeds, bringing
Cowslips and other small plants out of the mould, changing
The barren shale to faerie, coaxing
Mica glints out of the flat, unappreciative sidewalks,
Turning everything around but making it
Delightful), occupied as they are
With furthering their own desires, spreading
Their dominion over the flat, quiet land around them.
But no one is punished for inattention any more:
It seems, in fact, to further the enjoyable
Side of the world's activities. What seemed
Reckless, incoherent, even filthy at times
Is now the shortest distance; everything gets done
And, more important, ought to be done
This way, and only in this way,
For happiness to sustain, and fish to remain
In the depths, not elbowing the birds of the skies;
For it all to come right and not be noticed

Mindful of teasing and subtle pressures put,
Yet careful to seize the pen first. "What
Have you been up to?" Well, this time has been very good
For my working, the work is progressing, and so
I assume it's been good for you too, whose work
Is also doubtless coming along, indeed, I know so
From the sudden aging visible in both of us, tired
And cozy around the eyes, as the work prepares to take off.

Anyway, I am the author. I want to
Talk to you for a while, teach you
About some things of mine, some things
I've put away, more still that I remember
With a tinge of sadness, even
Regret around the sunset hour, that puts these
Things away, jettisons 'em, pulls the plug
On 'em, the carpet out from under their feet:
Even such, they say, as stand in narrow lanes
Wanly soliciting passersby, but without much
Hope of interest. Nevertheless, the
Things I want to visit with you about
Are important to me. I've kept them so long!

Zephyrs are one. How
Idly they played around me, around
My wrists, even in the bygone time!

And pictures—
Pictures of capes and peninsulas
With big clouds moving down on them,
Pressing with a frightening weight—

Until just after it has slipped by, for the noble
And wonderful thing it is, so that the other
Visions may arise and occupy the same space.

Before long they too
Turn up in your mind.
You wonder what the original uses
Of famine were, after
We saw the film about it.
The brine shrimp were brought
And the fairy pudding placed next to them.
It's good though—
It has meat on it.

We fucked too long,
Though, you see.
Now it's too late to stay home
Or go anywhere except to that film
We've both seen a dozen or more times.
Of course it's good—that's why
We saw it so often—
But after a while one feels one has lived it
And wants to get on with other living experiences.
Yet we keep returning to it—
It is good, after all, and we know the plot
And the characters by now, which makes it
Ours in a way that living our own lives
Never does. We know ourselves
And each other only too well; on the other
Hand the action is always new, though plotless,
The same. Toes are again pointed

And shipwrecks barely seen (sometimes
Not seen at all) through the snow
In the foreground, and howling, ravenous gales
In the background. Almost all landscapes
Are generous, well proportioned, hence
Welcome. We feel we have more in common with a
Landscape, however shifty and ill-conceived,
Than with a still-life: those oranges
And apples, and dishes, what have they to do
With us? Plenty, but it's a relief
To turn away from them. Portraits, on the other
Hand, are a different matter—they have no
Bearing on the human shape, their humanitarian
Concerns are foreign to us, who dream
And know not we are humane, though, as seen
By others, we are. But this is about people.
Right. That's why landscapes are more
Familiar, more what it's all about—we can see
Into them and come out on the other side. With
People we just see another boring side of ourselves,
One we may not know too well, but on the other
Hand why should we be interested in it? Better
The coffee pot and sewing basket of a still-life—
It's more human, if you want, I mean something
A human is more likely to be interested in
Than pictures of human beings, no matter how well drawn
And sympathetic-looking. However, as the author
Of this, I want to buy a certain picture,
A still-life in fact, from a man who has one
And need the permission of the man
In order to do so. Unless I can acquire it

Down a sidewalk, spring
Is in the air and the word "brothel" floats
Like a ribbon in the sunset, upsetting
The teen balance that was never anything
But a continuing collapse, that brought
Music and minor pleasures, and some
Nourishment, but always rolled back the conditions
To that flat, narrow time before the beginning,
Kind of a sample of the horizon
Before there was any place for it
And now that it exists it seems
Almost tame, or not as ripe
As we always imagined it would be.

In the sea of the farm
The dream of hay whirls us toward
Horizons like those only
Imagined, with no space, no groove
Between the sky and the earth, metallic,
Unfleshed, as though, as children,
Each of us might say how good
He or she is, and afterwards it is forgotten,
The thought, the very words.

But there are times when darkness
Hides this not very real horizon, and it turns
Steadfast for us. Sprays
Of trees are imagined there, and they endure
For a while once daylight has come,
The stubborn, sticky mixture of daylight.

I can never feel the point of any of this. Oh,
I can see it intellectually, all right, but to really
Feel it, experience it, I have to have the picture.
That's all. I'd hate to give it up.

To be consigned to this world
Of life, a sea-world
Which forms, shapes,
Faces probably decorate—
It is all as you had suspected
All along, my dear.
They proliferate slowly, build,
Then clog, and in weathering
Become a foundation of sorts
For what is afterwards to be erected
On this plot of unfinal ecstasies—
Benign, in sum. They don't just go away, either.
But like a hollow tower
Let in some sun, and keep the wind
Far hence; whatever can destroy
Us loses, but it's pretty hard to say
How far we have come, how much accomplished
And whether there's a lot more to be said:
But for stretches at a time of life the outlined
Masks and scabbards which are our vague
Impression of what is probably going on
All around us, keep us distracted,
From playing and working too hard.
And yet life is not really for the squeamish either.
The hyacinths are dying
At the end of a broad blue day

If all the retinues of all
The archdukes stretched away into a powdery
Infinity, and you stood
On the top step but one, waiting to advance
Your argument into the aura, and time suddenly
At that moment seemed to sag, and the staircase
Became a giant hammock littered with dead leaves
And ants, and the horizon of the universe
Raised it up into something bald and filled
With unexpressed and inexpressible menace,
No word of which would ever
Attest to the configuration of desires
That had gone into its construction, dark now,
Absent-minded flowers, reticent birds, and much
Else that is scarcely present, needing
No avenue, no way to be born,
Who would greet you? Which might be
What you want to tell me: open the door.

Your hopes and fears, ambitions, inspirations
Are a closed book to me. And your
Uneasy acceptance of what doesn't really matter,
Like a makeshift latrine, is, well,
Changed back into remoteness by your verbs
Like winking dragonflies that officiate
So far down near the bottom of "caring"
As to seem interlopers, themselves
Displaced by later arrivals
That fell off the others, are part
And parcel, but that merely, of

Whose words somehow have not touched you.

Mad to sacrifice next to them
In late life, you were "just looking"
Instead when the uneasy feeling that a jewel
Might someday be around crossed you
But I can't figure out
What ever happened. You treasured it,
I contain you, and there are a few clouds
Down near the baseboard of the room that prevent
Us from ever continuing our conversation
About the terrible lake that exists behind us.
Piss and destruction
Are the order of the day, the office blues,
The Monday morning smiling through tears
That never come.

Partly because you always expect the impossible,
But also because here, on the level of personal
Life, it becomes easier to say, nay, think
The transversals that haven't stopped
Defining our locus, have indeed only begun
To, you are invited, and cannot refuse,
To share this wall
Of painted wooden tulips, the wooden clouds
In the sky behind it, to feel the intensity
As it is there. Good news travels fast
But what about the news you forgot
To tell until now, so we can't tell
All that much about it? Well, it joins us.
The ground is soaked with tears.

The old, old wonderful story:
Grace and linearity
That take us up and bathe us, changing
The dirty colors of the little zephyrs
Into the next best thing: short gaffer,
Very short roses.

It goes without saying that I can't,
"For the life of me," figure out why we were both
Here. You are again listening to Haydn quartets,
Following them with the score. Afterwards
I wander all over you. Anyway that is the
Way I want you, the way things are
Going to be increasingly.

"Now to my tragic business."
The moon, in a coma, listens nevertheless
To all that is said. Any word we
May have ever uttered gets recorded and
Catalogued, and anybody can go and look them up.
The storms don't matter; even when the wind
Is about to demolish the roof, and the sea
Is banging on the front door, our words,
Even whispers, even unuttered thoughts are
Channeled into this cesspool of oral history.
You may be wondering about what comes next.

Never change when love has found its home.

Compliments of "a friend."

The tears of centuries are being wiped away.
The tower is beaded with sweat that
Has smiled down on our effort
For so long.

The lovers saunter away.
It is a mild day in May.
With music and birdsong alway
And the hope of love in the way
The sleeve detaches itself from the body
As the two bodies do from the throng of gay
Lovers on the prowl that do move and sway
In the game of sunrise they play
For stakes no higher than the gray
Ridge of loam that protects the way
Around the graveyard that sexton worm may
Take to the mound Death likes to stay
Near so as to be able to slay
The lovers who humbly come to pray
Him to pardon them yet his stay
Of execution includes none and they lay
Hope aside and soon disappear.

Yet none is in disrepair
And soon, no longer in fear
Of the flowers their arrears
Vanish and each talks gaily of his fear
That is in the past whose ear
Has been pierced by the flowers and the air
Is now contagious to him.

But not in our day. It sits
Open and limited like the yard.

Yet there are silent beginnings of beginnings,
Nothing but prayers, though it seems
That we can now feel with our minds
Which is someplace between prayers
And the answer to prayers.

In all these
Accessories of going down into day, though polished
And bristling, the telling of the way
Still fails to appear. Stopping everyone
Along the way for news of a long list
Of people, the field of folk
Is full of people in gentle raiment
Of the sun woven with the moon, and smiles
Half hilarious and half tragic, so that they
Seem specters of some cosmic romance
Beyond comedy and tragedy, and their love pours
Over the dikes and barriers that are no more
Now that the flood has occurred
And stopped, a broad and quiet ocean
Woven of the sun and wind and true
Kisses that are heartier than love.

Kind words are like apples of gold
And pitchers of silver.

I thought I thought I thought

He walks by the sea wall
With a mate or lover and all
The waves stand on tiptoe around the ball
Of land where they all are.

Thus, by giving up much,
The lovers have lost less than
The average man.

No bird of paradise flies up
With an explosive cry at his touch,
The lover's, yet all
Are made whole in the circle that rounds
Him, filled the whole time with sweet sounds.

It is not the disrepair of these lives
Where we may find the key to all that gives
Eloquence and truth to our passing thoughts,
And shapes them as a shipwright shapes
The staves for the hull of some desolate
Ship; rather, it is in the disrepair
Of these lives that we not find despair
But all that nourishes and comforts death
In life and causes people to gather round
As when they hear a good story is being told
And makes us wish we were younger but also cherishes
Our advancing years, and to find there no fears.

The tower was more a tower inside a house.
Even its outside (tendril-clogged crannies)

In vain
At last I thought with my name.

Remember me now
Remember me ever
And think of the fun
We had together.

A friend.

I will tell you lovers, it is the little boy or sire
That has a present smell or word
For all their meat.

A little boy was running away
To be seen no more, who is now seen
As before, in the abstract and the particular,
The flesh and the appearance of flesh,
Who is not unlike the little boy
Of love, with his mama
The lady of love, who arranged all this
And who is good beyond the shadows
Of evil and corruption others throw
Into our corner but we are always beside them.

Some think him mean-tempered and gruff
But actually his is an occasion for all occasions
And one can get by calling anything love
As long as it's locked up in the Finis
Of the end, and still come out ahead.
(This is probably the fourth most important kind of love

Was shaded from the view of most.
It grew chaste, and slim, like a prism
In a protected, secular environment
That overlooked the torment, fogs and crevasses
Of orderly religion. That house
Grew all alone in a desolate avenue
(Avenue so shady)
That people began to forget coming to
Long before its present state
Of patched-up oblivion, and even
In those days were those who remembered back
To what seemed a state of true freedom:
Bopping down the valleys wild, beaks
Tearing the invisible ear to shreds
But was actually a rudimentary stage
Of serfdom dating from the Silver Age.
Now, however, that house was as it was
Never going to be: a modest yet firmly
Rooted pure excrescence, a spiritual
Rubber plant:
A grave no one wanted to visit
Which remained popular and holy down to the present
    afternoon,
Something which nobody in particular
Was interested in, yet which mattered more
To the earth's population in general
Than practically anything they could think of.
It was history just as it disappears in the
Twilight of yesterday and before it
Materializes today as everything that is
Fresh, young, and strange, and almost

But as long as lovers still look at the moon
In June, weaving fingers under the moon
We cannot know what happens here,
Whether or not we should go away.)

But I'm against all forms of physical
Sexual activity—against billy goats, too,
Never could stand 'em. Which is why
It's difficult to get up in public and proclaim
About my cherished sorrow departing,
My appetite coming back, since all lovers
Are shadows projected from behind on the screen
Of my collective unconscious, eidolons
That won't say yes or no, but keep prodding
The ground for the treasure buried there.

One or two a year is all right
But more than that releases the shadow
Of throngs of passersby, of the correct object
And the precise moment in the sea-level street.
So later we come to abide
By the state as we remember it
And in dreams overhear it
And all our richness of invention
Is as physic to the evil of the surround
Which can't exist until we go after it,
Prove it by default.
Therefore I can't advance too much
Toward the packed, glittering crowd:
It dematerializes too soon and my oblivion
Is the cost of the precise definition there

Out of the house and halfway down the street—
An index, in other words, of everything
That is not going to and is going to happen
To us once we forget about its progress
And actually begin to feel better
For having done so.

It goes without saying that
To have it make sense you
Would have to belong to all who are asleep
Making no sense, and then
Flowers of the desert begin, peep by peep,
To emerge and you are saved
Without having taken a step, but I
Don't know how you're going to get
Another person to do that. It all boils down to
Nothing, one supposes. There is a central crater
Which is the word, and around it
All the things that have names, a commotion
Of thrushes pretending to have hatched
Out of the great egg that still hasn't been laid.
These one gets to know, and by then
They have formed tightly compartmented, almost feudal
Societies claiming kinship with the word:
(If on a priority basis however
It takes longer to catch them)
And their age flows out of time, is left
Like a bluish deposit on the brown ploughed fields
That surround our century: like the note of a harp.

The phosphorescent spring fails, and newer,

Besides which no one would ever want to see it
In that much detail (warts and all)
Knowing he would have to come out that way
Himself one day, and turn his back on all
He had with such difficulty become,
A pejorative lover, alone and palely
Loitering, having forgotten what the object
Of his affection was, with only the Pavlovian
Reflex of loving left to try to remind him
What it was all like one day, how it could have
Been. And as we realize this, they
Grow paler but more fixed, more sovereign
For this day and this hour, are what
Has been bearing down all along, the sleep
We have tried without success to ward off
All day, until the trap
Of night caves in under us and we emerge
Pellucid and dry-eyed as the others, beings made of
Love and time, who are to each other
What each is to himself.

I cry in the daytime,
And in the night season, and am not silent.
But what shall clean me within?
The way to nothing
Is the way to all things. The thoroughfare
That kept me inside
Is blocked with thurifers
That would lead to a different kind of life.
Yet all behaviors
Are equal in the eyes of a jade leaf

Numbered days come up. The wind pulls at
The leaves of the calendar, peels them off one by one
In a fitful expression of what time is like
As it goes by, that's like a look
Out of a window, and then the moment has gone away
From the window. The vast quantities of scum
Did not materialize. Only the sterile minuet
Proceeds at an always altered rate
Leading to bad feelings here and there
But the main feeling is safe and out of reach.

Love is different.
It moves, or grows, at the same rate
As time does, yet within time:
The waxing is invisible, and can never be felt
Outside time, as a few things—happiness,
For instance—can. As perennial as time
Is, and as insipid to the tongue, yet it
Is built in another street; such luminescence
As it has, it takes from the idea of itself
Each of us has, and knows not, except
To recognize, and feel secure again about its growing:
I mean that it is a replica
Of itself, which is itself the replica,
Counterfeited from itself, which is something
False, yet true, like the moon, and whose
Earthly reflection is of a truly
Hair-raising solidity, like the earth
Dissolved in the sun, suffused with a kinetic
Purpose it could never have for us
Unless we dreamed it. It is, then,

Prodded into history
But with a sense of itself and of society
Unequal to history.

History is a forest
In which a separate, positioned leaf
Could not occur
Leading to storms as multitudinous and varied
As the drops in a single storm
That flowers by the roadside
In winter, as white is taken this way
As an object which the mind can never
Control, leading to frosted silence
And cold unregard.

It is a landmark in a chain of landmarks,
Never to be harvested.

The atrocious accident, as ascribed
In columns of print, refreshes,
And briefly, but the memory
Of its signification does not go away.
Instead of forgetting, we become nicer.

After which it is time to play.

The Yellow River (the river,
Not the novel by I. P. Daly) has suffered a
Decline in popularity, though it
Passes through one of the world's most
Populous regions. Think about it.

Gigantic, yet life-size. And
Once it has lived, one has lived with it. The astringent,
Clear timbre is, having belonged to one,
One's own, forever, and this
Despite the green ghetto that intrudes
Its blighted charm on each of the moments
We called on love for, to lead us
To farther tables and new, surprised,
Suffocated chants just beyond the range
Of simple perception. These, brown
Motes, may unclasp themselves like
Japanese paper flowers at any moment,
Rending themselves into a final
Fixed appreciation of themselves and whatever
They were going to be confronted with
Lest the politicians despair of its ever
Becoming a diamond that gives back the night
Into its smallest box and learns to live
With itself, like a true feeling.

On the heights, jammed with pagodas
And temples, the light
Is starting to recede, the popularity
That no one wants. But in the flat
Depths of the gorges, the river is waning
On. Now no one comes
To disturb the murk, and the profoundest
Tributaries are silent with the smell
Of being alone. How it
Dances alone, in winter shine
Or autumn filth. It is become
Ingrown, and with this
Passes out of our existence, as we enter
A new chapter, confused and possibly excited,
Yet a new one, all the same.

But, what is time, anyway? Not,
Not certainly, the faces and pleasures
Encrusted in it, the "beautifully varied streets,"
The wicked taunting us to some kind of action,
Any kind, with hands partially covering
Their faces, to hide or to mock us, or both.
No, these things are part of time,
Or are rather a kind of parallel tide,
A related activity. And the markings?

Some say that the measuring of time
Is a recognition of what it is, but
I think the things that are in it
Are more like it, though not quite it.

Actually what is in it is controlled
And colored by the units of measuring it.
That summer jog you had
A long time ago
Is probably it, it fits so
Neatly over it anyway, nobody
Could ever tell the difference.

And what was said
All afternoon, long afternoons
Ago, whatever it was, and it

But I want him here.
Something is changed without him,
Something we will go on understanding
Until he returns to us.

The sunset is no reflection
Of its not knowing—even its knowing
Can be known but is not
A reflection.

Sometimes when we see another person
Walking down a street or
Standing to one side, we feel
We ought to go up and speak to that person
Because they expected to die.
But we do not, or seldom, speak to strangers.

It is forbidden
To have much to do with strangers.
We can lie, and get along in short periods
That way, we can go out of our house
To see what is there, but we can
Turn around and go back and not speak
To the others who were there
No matter who they were.

Was something special, you know
You really can remember it.

I wanted to forget it but it was like
Not remembering it and having the whole
Force of it brought home to you, and who
Wants that? Who cares, anyway, about
What it is or what it was like?
You must be mad to care. Yes,
I am mad, I think, and I do care.
I can't help it. I am mad,
And don't care. But it will not remain
Any more outside of me for all that.
It is the marrow of my thought
That all night I stand up chewing,
Trying to remember things, mostly things
I'd forgotten, and who
Remembers these? And also
Some things I
Actually remembered, and here I am
Trying to remember them all over again, to have
Them live up to me.
And it is as it was when I was a kid:
The moment stays on, but is
Lacing up its shoelaces or engaged
In some other form of maddening and hard to
Notice activity, but it gets its work done,
And still it can stay it has stayed
Around long enough to count for that
So that it is I who have aged without
Having done anything, certainly nothing

We could feel ashamed, on some days
That it was all brought before
And we in it,
That we have not known an edict, and that
Person knows it too. We are seldom
Invited by friends, and even less by strangers.

That is the problem of having too many friends:
We forget most of them, and just
When we need them most, they are gone.
We have no friends at any given
Moment, or they are gone away.

However, we do have friends when we need them.
They are almost always around, the shore
Has them. The lake recedes
Toward the close, pale horizon like a bench.
We were not asked any more
And now we feel we have given up on them.
They will never rely on us
Even if we were to go down, all the way down,
To them. They might not like us any more.

But the sunset sees its reflection, and
In the curve
Is cured. People, not all, come back
To us in pairs or threes. And so
Are festive, the light in the face
And all people shoo

To deserve it, like a lost cause.

I would just love to go
Would love it
And you too want to go, with me,
And there is no reason not to, nothing
Keeping us here, we
Can go out into the street
Where nobody is, no dirt
Any more, and climb to the lower edge of the sky
And wait there, and soon
Someone will come to take care of us.

All I want
Is for someone to take care of me,
I have no other thought in mind,
Have never entertained any.
When that day comes I'll go gladly
Into whatever situation or room you want me in
To take care of.
And meanwhile I'll wait, obligingly, full
Of manna and joy, for that to take place
Which it will, soon.

But why you
May ask do I want someone to take care of me
So much? This is why:
I can do it better than anyone, and have
All my life, and now I am tired
And a little bored with taking care of myself
And would like to see how somebody else might

You, they are back on the place
Of the temple, and nothing seems rustic any more.

They have their own perfume though
And it keeps growing through the mist.
The trees—excuse me—keep smiling—are grown
In the comprehensive materials
That swim alternately over and under
Never appreciating any more
Never stopping to think
Or ask why things are this way
And not the way you thought they
Were going to be
                    which would have been nicer.
The light of some forgotten hell
Leaves them in a new state of mind, begging
The question of growth,
Of additional dampers.

The prettiness urges
Far into the body, deep
Into the coffin of reactions, splitting light
Into two unequal portions. One
For me, the other for my things
Like my memories and the changes I'd
Want to introduce each time I'd come to a
Particular one but would turn over instead,
Disappointed with the other way it'd
Turn out shoveling no matter what
Into the boiler to keep that engine going
And it would all reduce to this or that other

Do it, even if that person falls on their face
Trying to, in the attempt.
When leaves pass over, and then ice
And finally warm, bottled-up breezes
I'll notice how it has all seemed the same until now,
This very moment, and as a
Duck takes off into the nether blue,
Find my rationale or whatever, something
Inside these movements all around me that
Enclose me loosely like a cage with the bars
Wide enough apart to walk through
Into the open air, onto God's road, in the blond,
Shambling sunlight, and look back
After all that, thinking how fortunate
It has all been on the whole, and how, though joy
Has been lacking, and that severely on occasion,
Happiness has not. I must
Make do with happiness, and am glad
To do so, as long as everyone
Is happy and doesn't mind. The car
Drove back to get me, through miles and miles
Of mud ruts and mangrove swamps, and stopped
And I got in and it drove away
To a slightly less flat land where you
And I can build a new life together on the shore
Several inches above sea level as the blue
Whitecaps on the charging waves come foaming in.

The Americans, with a sigh, never call it
By another word than its name. O
People who loiter by the Pacific,

Blackened memory, always the same, always
Healthy in spite of it. O who
Can judge their memories lest they have
Already been sized up by them?

But it is April now,
An air of commerce in things, and I should
Forget the past and think about
The flutes and premises of the future, and whether
A satisfactory sex life was one of the things
Included in the agenda or somebody forgot it
Again—just like them—
And the life of art
Matters a lot now too, is seen
To be perhaps the most important of all, slightly
Overtopping that other, and joy
Is after all predestined. Isn't it? I mean
Otherwise, what the fuck are we doing
Here, worrying about it, having it all collapse
On our heads trying to dig our way out
Of this sand pit? No,
It's got to be preordained, in some way, by
Someone, otherwise we wouldn't like it,
Recognize it as it flies, and sit down casually
Again, knowing that, as the truth knows
A true story when it hears one, so we, wandering
Along the lake again shall hear blossoms
And imagine radiant blue flamingoes against the sacred sky.

As for those others, citizens
Of the great night, freaks, weirdos,

Whose swaggering insouciance might convince
If left to play, and who can never lie,
Not even from the truth, how is it
With you, nestling all of you on one side?
The buildup predicted by others never
Quite matriculated, and now some of you
Are in this impasse, preparing to stay, while
Others straggle here and there, finding
Food, shelter, deserts, and in the tall
Tales some kindling, an advantage, and
You never look down.

The narrator:
Something you would want here is the
Inexpressible, rage of form
Vs. content, to show how the latter,
The manner, vitiates the thing-in-
Itself that the poem is actually about
And which, for this reason, cannot
Be considered the subject. Living
On the tranquil slope of an inactive volcano
All these days which group themselves
Into decades, consuming
The egg puddings of each one of these days
Is like unto form as subject matter
Perceives it through the cracks in its
Makeshift cell, and knows
There is light and activity outdoors to which
It can never contribute, but of which
It must needs always be aware, and this
Oozing sore is the progress, slow

Commies and pimps: once it was all hers,
The Queen of Diamonds,
As they called her. Her real name
Was Rosine Esterhazy. That's what she thought.

Then the war was postponed.
The boyfriends flooded the fields.
She thought it was some protection
Nor was the great night considered especially
Dangerous.

The flower fields thriving
On craft items which can be made
At night. And for a few years, there is peace.
We can use this time for changing, shifting
Back to be a better way
Into ourselves. These years have become
A masquerade. Fine! We'll use that too,
Drinking toasts to perfect strangers.
When the winter is over, and the sodden spring
That goes on even longer, a pitcher of water
Drawn deep from the well is to be
The reward and the end of just about everything,
And joy invades all this. Makes it
Hard to write about.

Just a few letters lately, in fact,
Choruses of praise from outsiders, and I keep
Dropping my diary different places, forgetting

And miserable at times but magnificent
In its conception, in theory, and may never
Be anything more than this, but knows
About itself. Luckily, the object
Keeps making itself known to the opinions
About form and remains strong and warm
Long after it has gone out of fashion
And so never ceases, even in its earliest
Days preceding its demise, to be a runic
Maquette of the ideal poem-construct
Even after it has finally washed its hands of all
Notion of form, pleads ignorance or conflict
Of interest, and releases Barabbas to the
Delighted distraction of the rabble whose
Destiny is always to be of two minds
About everything and will end up on your doorstep
If you don't watch out:
You private yet public excuse for a still
Active poetasting writer but whether what
Is lasting in your work will last is the
Big question: it's poetry, it's extraordinary,
It makes a great deal of sense. It starts out
With some notion and switches to both, yet
The object will be partially perceived by the forms
Around it it is responsible for.

Note that, in the liturgical sense
Of history, the way I see it, we are falling down
In our duty toward the dustman's spasms, derelict
And decrepit as regards the outside world.
Deduce a spasm? Aye, a very

What I was talking about, letting it combine
With the loam and humus, and maybe a quick
Star-shape of a flower is produced. If not,
Each of us still has all our work to be done
In the joy of working so that the even greater joy
Of the hammock may be tasted later on, and so much
Of the padding may be appreciated then for what it is,
Just stuffing, of the kind that is needed
Everywhere, that keeps the Mozart symphonies
Apart and gradually leads us, each of us,
Back to the fragment of sense which is the place
We started out from. Isn't it strange
That this was home all along, and none of us
Knew it? What could our voyages
Have been like, that we forgot them so soon,
What galleons, what freighters were made to appear
And as sullenly to vanish in the thick foam bearing
Down from the horizon? What kind of a school
Is this, that they teach you these things,
And neglect whatever was important, that we were made to
     feel
Around for and so lost our names
And our dogs and were coming back, back
Into the commotion under the waterwheels
So that everything is spinning now, bears
Very little resemblance to what was supposed to be the
     entrance to the port, but is now
Whittled away to almost nothing?

But I wouldn't want you to think I
Cared for anything rather than go home

Insomniac'd tear it down so as to rebuild
And resell it. Tear his tattered ensign
Down? I don't know, I thought it looked nice
Hanging overhead, though I could
Be wrong. Valentine, I need you,
The mice in the plaster disturb all my reasoning
On this vale, this slope. The outer districts
Were succinct, full of enough plans,
But on the interior was the abysm, no
Invitation available, nothing about
The plodding fever that grew him, and the worries
That came after. No clue.
In industry we are persuaded that we may in some
Connection contribute a certain stone or effort
And this lazily winds away over the hill.

Or say that between the effort and the screws
Some scorpion intruded, and to top
It off a storm interfered with the rescue efforts
Blurring them? What then? What do you make
Of the red traffic light turning green to admit
A few cars farther on in the shuffle when night
Binds the tubing with rain and you
Can see yourself only as you used to be in college?
Make you mine
Valentine
Feelin' fine too if consumed
With energy to be mad and go on
Confessing even if it means that the sought-after
Absolution be rescinded after a time and those who
Looked silently at you for a while direct

In the rain to the crafty islet
With the gasoline under the cellar
Roof. Yet betimes
In the morning stuck with the
Magic of turning into everything
Insane amid chimes he breathes and preaches,
Envy of all but himself. Silent,
The parishioners file out, leaving the last man
On the quasi-tropical islet; he is left
As if alone again. No one cares
For its train—what greasy pebbles and rocks
It slithered over occupy
No one's attention any more and much
More is in store for the hyenas coupling
In the wallpaper and much less will have been
Noted down about this once he returns,
If ever. We clarify everything,
Throw it away and then the ranch comes
To devour our after-need, and what
Is left is of the kind no one uses.

Some certified nut
Will try to tell you it's poetry,
(It's extraordinary, it makes a great deal of sense)
But watch out or he'll start with some
New notion or other and switch to both
Leaving you wiser and not emptier though
Standing on the edge of a hill.
We have to worry
About systems and devices there is no
Energy here no spleen either

Their gaze downward to the sunlit
Tundra. And you go out to the party
As toes slip into shoes
And I am not just left on the corner
But am as the traveling salesman of a joke
With a permanent hard-on and no luck and
All these samples in this here suitcase. Wanna see 'em?
Otherwise, why, we don't know too much. Fellow was over
Here recently from the British Isles
Wanted to see something of how the life goes
On. He never made it back. Well some of us
Enjoy that way too as though we knew
Life was a picnic or parade down under the
Hassles and disrobing, the dust,
But now well we pretend to see otherwise
Into the great blue eyes of concrete that best
Our city, in the time of industry, and so
Panic slowly in the vegetal heart of things
Until told to disconnect the operation.
No wonder so many of us
Get discouraged, know not where to turn.

The truth is that nowhere in Europe,
India or America is this a straight line
Drawn, vertically, from one point to another
So as to connect them and in so doing
Provide a lot of fun and refreshment
For the students so they may never
Feel insecure again. Such a line may exist
But it would be horizontal, like the Northwest Passage,
And not connect people up with anything else.

We have to take over the sewer plans—
Otherwise the coursing clear water, planes
Upon planes of it, will have its day
And disappear. Same goes for business:
Holed up in some office skyscraper it's
Often busy to predict the future for business plans
But try doing it from down
In the street and see how far it gets you! You
Really have to sequester yourself to see
How far you have come but I'm
Not going to talk about that.

I'm fairly well pleased
With the way you and I have come around the hill
Ignoring and then anointing its edge even if
We felt it keenly in the backwind.
You were a secretary at first until it
Came time to believe you and then the black man
Replaced your headlights with fuel
You seemed to grow from no place. And now,
Calmed down, like a Corinthian column
You grow and grow, scaling the high plinths
Of the sky.

Others, the tenor, the doctor,
Want us to walk about on it to see how we feel
About it before they attempt anything, yet
In whose house are we? Must we not sit
Quietly, for we would not do this at home?
A splattering of trumpets against the very high

It's a wager, and emptiness, and though warm
And the color of baked loaves in the sun
It has no idea of nourishment or where
You should go.

Its idea is that the Latin text
Might also have existed in German or be so close
It doesn't matter any more and the cottage
Be shut up at the end of summer and be there
Come early or mid-spring, but this
Presupposes a helpless mankind pigeonholed
With a rival deity so that neither can make
The hands of the clock move and it all goes down
In darkness, with the sun. To the supreme
Moment then, but it spreads out in sullenness
Over a vast tidal plain to dissipate in what
It is not even sure is horizon, is nothing but
Images. Earthly inadequacy
Is indescribable, and heavenly satisfaction
Needs no description, but between
Them, hovering like Satan on airless
Wing is the matter at hand:
The essence of it is that all love
Is imitative, creative, and that we can't hear it.

Oh, once
A long time ago, in towns and cities
The line was different. We lived
Indifferently then, but perhaps more accurately,
And once it was over we knew
What to do with it. We carried out

Pockmarked wall and a forgetting of spiny
Palm trees and it is over for us all,
Not just us, and yet on the inside it was
Doomed to happen again, over and over, like a
Wave on a beach, that thinks it's had this
Tremendous idea, coming to crash on the beach
Like that, and it's true, it has, yet
Others have gone before, and still others will
Follow, and far from undermining the spiciness
Of this individual act, this knowledge plants
A seed of eternal endeavor for fear of
Happening just once, and goes on this way,
And yet the originality should not deter
Our vision from the drain
That absorbs, night and day, all our equations,
Makes us brittle, emancipated, not men in a word.
Dying of fright
In the violet night you come to understand how it
Looked to the ancestors and what there was about it
That moved them and are come no closer
To the divine riddle which is aging,
So beautiful in the eternal honey of the sun
And spurs us on to a higher pitch
Of elocution that the company
Will not buy, and so back to our grandstand
Seat with the feeling of having mended
The contrary principles with the catgut
Of abstract sleek ideas that come only once in
The night to be born and are gone forever after
Leaving their trace after the stitches have
Been removed but who is to say they are

Our neighbors' lives and they had our
Instructions about where to go. We lived
Inadequately, blushing, but we knew we were
On the outside and that only one thing
Prevented us from traveling inward, and that
Thing was our knowledge of how little we imagined
Everything. As though a door
Were enough to stop the average person and he
Would just curl up on the doormat forever.

But this
Person turned out to be mass-produced. He was funny
And knew about elegance, how to dress
For an occasion, yet the error that incites us
To duplication was missing, or inexact. We have
Not spoken to him. It should be outrageous
To do so. Yet to ignore him will bring no light.

But to get it right
We might ask this once: how goes it
Down there? What objects
Have you found recently?

"There are no trade winds. The ocean too
Is someone's idea. The pleasant banter of
The elements cannot disguise this basically
Thin concept, nor remove us from
Contemplation of it, and that is the best
Answer that may precede the question. Until later
When the shooting fires light up the sides
Of the volcano and each task and catastrophe

Traces of what really went on and not
Today's palimpsest? For what
Is remarkable about our chronic reverie (a watch
That is always too slow or too fast)
Is the lively sense of accomplishment that haloes it
From afar. There is no need
To approach closely, it will be done from here
And work out better, you'll see.

So the giant slabs of material
Came to be, and precious little else, and
No information about them but that was all right
For the present century. Later on
We'd see how it might be in some other
Epoch, but for the time being it was neither
Your nor the population's concern, and may
Have glittered as it declined but for now
It would have to do, as any magic
Is the right kind at the right time.
There is no soothsaying
Yet it happens in rows, windrows
You call them in your far country.

But you are leaving:
Some months ago I got an offer
From Columbia Tape Club, Terre
Haute, Ind., where I could buy one
Tape and get another free. I accept-
Ed the deal, paid for one tape and
Chose a free one. But since I've been

Become clear and succinct. By that time kindness
Will have replaced effort."

Why keep on seeding the chairs
When the future is night and no one knows what
He wants? It would probably be best though
To hang on to these words if only
For the rhyme. Little enough,
But later on, at the summit, it won't
Matter so much that they fled like arrows
From the taut string of a restrained
Consciousness, only that they mattered.
For the present, our not-knowing
Delights them. Probably they won't be devoured
By the lions, like the others, but be released
After a certain time. Meanwhile, keep
Careful count of the rows of windows overlooking
The deep blue sky behind the factory: we'll need them.

Repeatedly billed for my free tape.
I've written them several times but
Can't straighten it out—would you
Try?

II ❀

SLEEPING IN THE CORNERS
OF OUR LIVES

So the days went by and the nickname caught on.

It became a curiosity, but it wasn't curious.
Afternoon leaves blew against the stale brick
Surface. Just an old castle. Enjoy it
While you're here. And in looking for a more convenient
    way
To save one's soul, one is led up to it like a season,
And in looking all around, and about, its tome
Becomes legible in the interstices. A great biography
That is also a good autobiography, at the station;
A honeycomb of pages with listings
Of the tried and true, that radiates
Out into what is there, that averages up as wind,
And settles back into a tepid, modest
Chamber with its mouse-gray furniture, its redundant
    pictures.

This is tall sleeping
To prepare you for the soup and the ruins
In giving the very special songs of the first meaning,
The ones incorporating the changes.

SILHOUETTE

Of how that current ran in, and turned
In the climate of the indecent moment
And became an act,
I may not tell. The road
Ran down there and was afterwards there
So that no further borrowing
Of criticism or the desire to add pleasure
Was ever seen that way again.

In the white mouths
Of your oppressors, however, much
Was seen to provoke. And the way
Though discontinuous, and intermittent, sometimes
Not heard of for years at a time, did,
Nonetheless, move up, although, to his surprise
It was inside the house,
And always getting narrower.

There is no telling to what lengths,
What mannerisms and fictitious subterranean
Flowerings next to the cement he might have
Been driven. But it all turned out another way.
So cozy, so ornery, tempted always,
Yet not thinking in his 1964 Ford
Of the price of anything, the grapes, and her tantalizing
    touch

So near that the fish in the aquarium
Hung close to the glass, suspended, yet he never knew her
Except behind the curtain. The catastrophe
Buried in the stair carpet stayed there
And never corrupted anybody.
And one day he grew up, and the horizon
Stammered politely. The sky was like muslin.
And still in the old house no one ever answered the bell.

MANY WAGONS AGO

At first it was as though you had passed,
But then no, I said, he is still here,
Forehead refreshed. A light is kindled. And
Another. But no I said

Nothing in this wide berth of lights like weeds
Stays to listen. Doubled up, fun is inside,
The lair a surface compact with the night.
It needs only one intervention,

A stitch, two, three, and then you see
How it is all false equation planted with
Enchanting blue shrubbery on each terrace
That night produces, and they are backing up.

How easily we could spell if we could follow,
Like thread looped through the eye of a needle,
The grooves of light. It resists. But we stay behind, among
   them,
The injured, the adored.

AS WE KNOW

All that we see is penetrated by it—
The distant treetops with their steeple (so
Innocent), the stair, the windows' fixed flashing—
Pierced full of holes by the evil that is not evil,
The romance that is not mysterious, the life that is not life,
A present that is elsewhere.

And further in the small capitulations
Of the dance, you rub elbows with it,
Finger it. That day you did it
Was the day you had to stop, because the doing
Involved the whole fabric, there was no other way to appear.
You slid down on your knees
For those precious jewels of spring water
Planted on the moss, before they got soaked up
And you teetered on the edge of this
Calm street with its sidewalks, its traffic,

As though they are coming to get you.
But there was no one in the noon glare,
Only birds like secrets to find out about
And a home to get to, one of these days.

The light that was shadowed then
Was seen to be our lives,
Everything about us that love might wish to examine,

Then put away for a certain length of time, until
The whole is to be reviewed, and we turned
Toward each other, to each other.
The way we had come was all we could see
And it crept up on us, embarrassed
That there is so much to tell now, really now.

FIGURES IN A LANDSCAPE

What added note, what responsibility
Do you bring? Inserted around us like birdcalls
With an insistent fall. But the body
Builds up a resistance. The signs
Are no longer construed as they could have been.

The yellow chevron sails against the blue block
Of the sky, and is off. It turns tail and disappears.

Moving through much tepid machinery,
It makes more sense as it goes along.
Father and the others will be there
In their wooden jewelry, under the trees,

Since it makes sense not to quarrel
About the hole. You will perhaps see us dancing
Whom no one could ever figure out until you settled
At our feet like bushes and in the new glare
Several of the old features returned.
Without that we'd shoot back into the hills.

STATUARY

The prevailing winds lied in intent
The day she was given up.
The long cloth cawed from the cough cave:
First shallow groping outward, thirsty bites, more
Than heart can bestow.

You tell me I missed the most interesting part
But I think I found the most interesting part:
An unheralded departure by extinguished torchlight
Whose decorative patina
Is everything to the group—wind, fire, breathing, snores.

I was not there I was aware of Yogi Bear
There where I found a most interesting port
Crying wares to millennial crossings of voyagers
But this space is a checkerboard,
Whether it be land, sea or art
Trapped in the principle of the great beyond
Lacking only the expertise to
"Make a statement."

OTHERWISE

I'm glad it didn't offend me
Not astral rain nor the unsponsored irresponsible musings

Of the soul where it exists
To be fed and fussed over
Are really what this trial is about.

It is meant to be the beginning
Yet turns into anthems and bell ropes
Swaying from landlocked clouds
Otherwise into memories.

Which can't stand still and the progress
Is permanent like the preordained bulk
Of the First National Bank

Like fish sauce, but agreeable.

FIVE PEDANTIC PIECES

An idea I had and talked about
Became the things I do.

The poem of these things takes them apart,
And I tremble. Sparse winter, less vulnerable
Than deflated summer, the nests of words.

Some of the tribes believe the spirit
Is immanent in a person's nail parings.
They gather up their dead swiftly,
At sundown. And this will be
Some forgotten day three years ago:
Startling evidence of light after death.

Another person. The yellow-brick and masonry
Wall, deeper, duller all afternoon
And a voice waltzing, fabricating works
Of sentimental gadgetry—messes he'd cook up.

And the little hotel looked all right
And well lit, in the dark, on the flat
Beach behind the breakers, stiff, harmless.
And you are amazed that so much flimsy stuff
Stays erect, trapped in our mummery.

FLOWERING DEATH

Ahead, starting from the far north, it wanders.
Its radish-strong gasoline fumes have probably been
Locked into your sinuses while you were away.
You will have to deliver it.
The flowers exist on the edge of breath, loose,
Having been laid there.
One gives pause to the other,
Or there will be a symmetry about their movements
Through which each is also an individual.

It is their collective blankness, however,
That betrays the notion of a thing not to be destroyed.
In this, how many facts we have fallen through
And still the old façade glimmers there,
A mirage, but permanent. We must first trick the idea
Into being, then dismantle it,
Scattering the pieces on the wind,
So that the old joy, modest as cake, as wine and friendship
Will stay with us at the last, backed by the night
Whose ruse gave it our final meaning.

HAUNTED LANDSCAPE

Something brought them here. It was an outcropping of
    peace
In the blurred afternoon slope on which so many picnickers
Had left no trace. The hikers then always passed through
And greeted you silently. And down in one corner

Where the sweet william grew and a few other cheap plants
The rhythm became strained, extenuated, as it petered out
Among pots and watering cans and a trowel. There were no
People now but everywhere signs of their recent audible
    passage.

She had preferred to sidle through the cane and he
To hoe the land in the hope that some day they would grow
    happy
Contemplating the result: so much fruitfulness. A legend.
He came now in the certainty of her braided greeting,

Sunlight and shadow, and a great sense of what had been
    cast off
Along the way, to arrive in this notch. Why were the
    insiders
Secretly amused at their putting up handbills at night?
By day hardly anyone came by and saw them.

They were thinking, too, that this was the right way to begin
A farm that would later have to be uprooted to make way
For the new plains and mountains that would follow after
To be extinguished in turn as the ocean takes over

Where the glacier leaves off and in the thundering of surf
And rock, something, some note or other, gets lost,
And we have this to look back on, not much, but a sign
Of the petty ordering of our days as it was created and led us

By the nose through itself, and now it has happened
And we have it to look at, and have to look at it
For the good it now possesses which has shrunk from the
Outline surrounding it to a little heap or handful near the
    center.

Others call this old age or stupidity, and we, living
In that commodity, know how only it can enchant the dear
    soul
Building up dreams through the night that are cast down
At the end with a graceful roar, like chimes swaying out over

The phantom village. It is our best chance of passing
Unnoticed into the dream and all that the outside said
    about it,

Carrying all that back to the source of so much that was
   precious.
At one of the later performances you asked why they called
   it a "miracle,"

Since nothing ever happened. That, of course, was the
   miracle
But you wanted to know why so much action took on so
   much life
And still managed to remain itself, aloof, smiling and
   courteous.
Is that the way life is supposed to happen? We'll probably
   never know

Until its cover turns into us: the eglantine for duress
And long relativity, until it becomes a touch of red under
   the bridge
At fixed night, and the cries of the wind are viewed as
   happy, salient.
How could that picture come crashing off the wall when no
   one was in the room?

At least the glass isn't broken. I like the way the stars
Are painted in this one, and those which are painted out.

The door is opening. A man you have never seen enters the
   room.
He tells you that it is time to go, but that you may stay,

If you wish. You reply that it is one and the same to you.
It was only later, after the house had materialized elsewhere,
That you remembered you forgot to ask him what form the
   change would take.
But it is probably better that way. Now time and the land
   are identical,

Linked forever.

MY EROTIC DOUBLE

He says he doesn't feel like working today.
It's just as well. Here in the shade
Behind the house, protected from street noises,
One can go over all kinds of old feeling,
Throw some away, keep others.
                              The wordplay
Between us gets very intense when there are
Fewer feelings around to confuse things.
Another go-round? No, but the last things
You always find to say are charming, and rescue me
Before the night does. We are afloat
On our dreams as on a barge made of ice,
Shot through with questions and fissures of starlight
That keep us awake, thinking about the dreams
As they are happening. Some occurrence. You said it.

I said it but I can hide it. But I choose not to.
Thank you. You are a very pleasant person.
Thank you. You are too.

I MIGHT HAVE SEEN IT

The person who makes a long-distance phone call
Is talking into the open receiver at the other end
The mysterious discourse also emerges as pointed
In his ear there are no people in the room listening

As the curtain bells out majestically in front of the starlight
To whisper the words This has already happened
And the footfalls on the stair turn out to be real
Those of your neighbor I mean the one who moved away

THE HILLS AND SHADOWS
OF A NEW ADVENTURE

Even the most finicky would find
Some way to stand in the way.
He looked down at the ledge,

Grappling with more serious, better times.
A lady's leg crossed his mind.
Far out at sea the gulls shifted like weights.

This freshness was only a chore. In other words
The screen of lights is always there, calling
A name of vowels and then there is silence,

A burnt-out moon, our old Franklin
Parked in the yard
Under the final shade.

If there was a way to separate these objects
We feel, from these lived eventualities
That torment our best intentions

With a vision of a man bent over his desk,
Writing, communicating with the pad
Which becomes dream velvet the next time,

A moonlit city in which minorities
Fluctuate, drawing out the cultural medium
As fine as floating threads of cobwebs

Around the one ambiguous space:
Its own discoverer and name,
Named after itself,

Which is its name, and all these go into cities
Like ships behind a sea wall.
You cannot know them

Yet they are a part of you, the cold reason part
You do know about.
You were not present at the beginning

But this is not so difficult to figure out:
Messengers crying your name
In the streets of all the principal cities.

Morning. An old tractor.
It seems strange that there is no name for these
And that the night passages now seem so clear
Where you thought were only telephone wires
And the birds of strange rented buildings
In a place close to the north yet not north
With a strong smell of burlap,
A place to wait for, not in.

KNOCKING AROUND

I really thought that drinking here would
Start a new chain, that the soft storms
Would abate, and the horror stories, the
Noises men make to frighten themselves,
Rest secure on the lip of a canyon as day
Died away, and they would still be there the next morning.

Nothing is very simple.
You must remember that certain things die out for awhile
So that they can be remembered with affection
Later on and become holy. Look at Art Deco
For instance or the "tulip mania" of Holland:
Both things we know about and recall
With a certain finesse as though they were responsible
For part of life. And we congratulate them.

Each day as the sun wends its way
Into your small living room and stays
You remember the accident of night as though it were a
    friend.
All that is forgotten now. There are no
Hard feelings, and it doesn't matter that it will soon
Come again. You know what I mean. We are wrapped in
What seems like a positive, conscious choice, like a bird
In air. It doesn't matter that the peonies are tipped in soot
Or that a man will come to station himself each night

Outside your house, and leave shortly before dawn,
That nobody answers when you pick up the phone.
You have all lived through lots of these things before
And know that life is like an ocean: sometimes the tide is
    out
And sometimes it's in, but it's always the same body of
    water
Even though it looks different, and
It makes the things on the shore look different.
They depend on each other like the snow and the
    snowplow.

It's only after realizing this for a long time
That you can make a chain of events like days
That more and more rapidly come to punch their own
    number
Out of the calendar, draining it. By that time
Space will be a jar with no lid, and you can live
Any way you like out on those vague terraces,
Verandas, walkways—the forms of space combined with
    time
We are allowed, and we live them passionately,
Fortunately, though we can never be described
And would make lousy characters in a novel.

NOT ONLY / BUT ALSO

Having transferred the one to the other
And living on the plain of insistent self-knowledge
Just outside the great city, I see many
Who come and go, and being myself involved in distant
    places

Ask how they adjust to
The light that rains on the traveler's back
And pushes out before him. It is always "the journey,"
And we are never sure if these are preparations
Or a welcome back to the old circle of stone posts

That was there before the first invention
And now seems a place of vines and muted shimmers
And sighing at noon
As opposed to

The terrain of stars, the robe
Of only that journey. You adjusted to all that
Over a long period of years. When we next set out
I had spent years in your company
And was now turning back, half amused, half afraid,

Having in any case left something important back home
Which I could not continue without,
An invention so simple I could never figure out
How they spent so many ages without discovering it.
I would have found it, altered it
To be my shape, probably in my own lifetime,
In a decade, in just a few years.

TRAIN RISING OUT OF
THE SEA

It is written in the Book of Usable Minutes
That all things have their center in their dying,
That each is discrete and diaphanous and
Has pointed its prow away from the sand for the next trillion
    years.

After that we may be friends,
Recognizing in each other the precedents that make us truly
    social.
Do you hear the wind? It's not dying,
It's singing, weaving a song about the president saluting the
    trust,

The past in each of us, until so much memory becomes an
    institution,
Through sheer weight, the persistence of it, no,
Not the persistence, that makes it seem a deliberate act
Of duration, much too deliberate for this ingenuous being

Like an era that refuses to come to an end or be born again.
We need more night for the sky, more blue for the daylight
That inundates our remarks before we can make them
Taking away a little bit of us each time

To be deposited elsewhere
In the place of our involvement
With the core that brought excessive flowering this year
Of enormous sunsets and big breezes

That left you feeling too simple
Like an island just off the shore, one of many, that no one
Notices, though it has a certain function, though an abstract
    one
Built to prevent you from being towed to shore.

LATE ECHO

Alone with our madness and favorite flower
We see that there really is nothing left to write about.
Or rather, it is necessary to write about the same old things
In the same way, repeating the same things over and over
For love to continue and be gradually different.

Beehives and ants have to be reexamined eternally
And the color of the day put in
Hundreds of times and varied from summer to winter
For it to get slowed down to the pace of an authentic
Saraband and huddle there, alive and resting.

Only then can the chronic inattention
Of our lives drape itself around us, conciliatory
And with one eye on those long tan plush shadows
That speak so deeply into our unprepared knowledge
Of ourselves, the talking engines of our day.

AND I'D LOVE YOU
TO BE IN IT

Playing alone, I found the wall.
One side was gray, the other an indelible gray.
The two sides were separated by a third,
Or spirit wall, a coarser gray. The wall
Was chipped and tarnished in places,
Polished in places.

I wanted to put it behind me
By walking beside it until it ended.
This was never done. Meanwhile
I stayed near the wall, touching the two ends.

With all of my power of living
I am forced to lie on the floor.
To have reached the cleansing end of the journey,
Appearances put off forever, in my new life
There is still no freedom, but excitement
Turns in our throats like woodsmoke.

In what skyscraper or hut
I'll finish? Today there are tendrils
Coming through the slats, and milky, yellowy grapes,
A mild game to divert the doorperson
And we are swiftly inside, the resurrection finished.

TAPESTRY

It is difficult to separate the tapestry
From the room or loom which takes precedence over it.
For it must always be frontal and yet to one side.

It insists on this picture of "history"
In the making, because there is no way out of the
   punishment
It proposes: sight blinded by sunlight.
The seeing taken in with what is seen
In an explosion of sudden awareness of its formal splendor.

The eyesight, seen as inner,
Registers over the impact of itself
Receiving phenomena, and in so doing
Draws an outline, or a blueprint,
Of what was just there: dead on the line.

If it has the form of a blanket, that is because
We are eager, all the same, to be wound in it:
This must be the good of not experiencing it.

But in some other life, which the blanket depicts anyway,
The citizens hold sweet commerce with one another
And pinch the fruit unpestered, as they will,

As words go crying after themselves, leaving the dream
Upended in a puddle somewhere
As though "dead" were just another adjective.

THE PRELUDES

The difficulty with that is
I no longer have any metaphysical reasons
For doing the things I do.
Night formulates, the rest is up to the scribes and the
    eunuchs.

The reasons though were not all that far away,
In the ultramarine well under the horizon,
And they were—why not admit it?—real,
If not all that urgent.
And night too was real. You could step up
Into the little balloon carriage and be conducted
To the core of bland festival light.
And you mustn't forget you can sleep there.

Over near somewhere else there is the problem
Of the difficulty. They weave together like dancers
And no one knows anything about the problem any more
Only the problem, like the outline
Of a housewife closing her door in the face of a traveling
    salesman
Throbs on the air for some time after.
Perhaps for a long time after that.

O we are all ushered in—
Into the presence that explains.

A BOX AND ITS CONTENTS

Even better than summer, but I no longer
Aim a poem at you, center of the forest at night,
One shoe off and one shoe on, half-nubile, old.
The excited ashes of your tale, always telling, more telling
Until the day we get it right,
A day of thoughtful joy. You said if it's all right

To do it then there will be animals sleeping under the trees
   anyway.
You come out of love. But are. The treasure they
Were firing at was always yours anyway, you meant
To stand for it. Now there is no way down. But we
Children of that particular time, we always get back down.
You see, only some of the others were crying
And how your broad smile paints in the wilderness
A scene of happiness, with balloons and cars.
It was always yours to dig into, and you can't, loving us.

THE CATHEDRAL IS

Slated for demolition.

I HAD THOUGHT THINGS
WERE GOING ALONG WELL

But I was mistaken.

OUT OVER THE BAY
THE RATTLE OF FIRECRACKERS

And in the adjacent waters, calm.

WE WERE ON THE TERRACE DRINKING GIN AND TONICS

When the squall hit.

FALLEN TREE

We do not have it, and they
Who have it are plunged in confusion:
It is so easy not to have it, the gold coin, *we* know
The contour of having it, a pocket
Around space that is an endless library
Where each book follows in a divinely ordered procession,
Like the rays of the sun.

Yet it was the pageant that you never wanted
But which you need now to make sense of the strengthening
Of the mounting days that begin to form a vault
Above this ancient red stage.
The days proceed.
Each is good in his role,
Very clever, in fact. But it is up to you
To make sense of what each has done.

Otherwise, in the rain-washed fiasco—
Twilight? A coming triumph? Or some other
Diversion you haven't yet learned to recognize?—
We shall never recognize our true reflections,
Speaking to them as strangers, scolding,
Asking the time of day.

And the love that has happened for us
Will not know us
Unless you climb to a median kingdom
Of no climate
Where day and night exist only for themselves
And the future is our table and chairs.

THE PICNIC GROUNDS

Let the music tell it:
It came here, was around for a little while,
And left, like the campers,
Leaving fire-blackened brick, wrappers of things
And especially monster mood and emptiness
Of those who were here and are gone.

A complex, but optional, experience.
Will the landscape mean anything new now?
But even if it doesn't, the charge
Is up ahead somewhere, in the near future,
Squashing even the allegory of the grass
Into the mould of its aura, a lush patina.

So we, with all our high-minded notions
Of the self and the eventually winged purpose
Of that self, are now meaning
The raw material of the days and the ways that came over.

The shadow has been indefinitely postponed.
And the shape it takes in the process
Of definition of the evolving
Delta of shapes is too far, far in the milky limpid
Future of things. Too far to care, yet

There are those who do care for that
Kind of outline, distant, yes, but warm,
Full of the traceable meaning that never
Gets adopted. Well, isn't that truth?

A SPARKLER

The simple things I notice:

That they were coming at us, were at us, and *were* us
In this night like rotten mayonnaise I am afraid of
(It is helping me out) and steady boys
I want no one to latch onto

This time it has a special snap

And how it curved outward that time was more elaborate
But in the end got fuzzier
And at the same time more deducible
An illuminated word entered its crucible

But just once come back see it the way
I now see it
Sit fooling with your hair
Looking at me out of the corner of your eye
I'm so sorry
For what we haven't done in the time we've known each
    other.

Then it's back to school
Again yes the sales are on.
What do you need? We'll try . . .

Or is it all just a symbol of bad taste,
Of a bad taste in the mouth? I tried,
Not hard but pretty regular. But the pitch was
Elsewhere, parallel. The habitués would have
Had it, entertained it anyway,
But I was in disgrace. I lived in disgrace.
I was no one on that lawn.

But, lasting by lasting,
And by no other moment, we have come down
At last to where the plumbing is.
We had hoped for a dialogue.
But they're rusty.

Then is it too late for me?
The wide angle that seeks to contain
Everything, as a sea, is an eye.
What is beheld is whatever lives,
Is wildly unappetizing and inappropriate,
And sits, and fits us.

THE WINE

It keeps a large supply of personal pronouns
On hand. They awaken to see
Themselves being used as it grows up,
Confused, in a rush of fluidity.

Once men came back here to rot.
Now the salt banners only interrupt the sky—
Black crystals, quartzite. The balm of not
Knowing living filters to the bottom of each eye.

The telephone was involved in it. And bored
Glances, boring questions about the hem no
One wanted to look at, or would admit having seen.
These things came after it was a place to go.

Yet nothing was its essence. The core
Remained as elusive as ever. Until the day you
Fitted the unlikely halves together, and they clicked.
So its wholeness was an order. But it had seemed not to

Be part of the original blueprint, the way
It had appeared in intermittent dreams, stretching
Over several nights, like that. But that was okay,
Providing the noise factor didn't suddenly loom

Too large, as was precisely happening just now.
Where have I seen that face before? And I see
Just what it means to itself, and how it came
Down to me. And so, in like manner, it came to be.

A LOVE POEM

And they have to get it right. We just need
A little happiness, and when the clever things
Are taken up (O has the mouth shaped that letter?
What do we have bearing down on it?) as the last thin curve
("Positively the last," they say) before the dark:
(The sky is pure and faint, the pavement still wet) and

The dripping is in the walls, within sleep
Itself. I mean there is no escape
From me, from it. The night is itself sleep
And what goes on in it, the naming of the wind,
Our notes to each other, always repeated, always the same.

THERE'S NO DIFFERENCE

In pendent tomes the unalterable recipe
Is decoded. Then, a space,
And another space. I was consulting
The surface of the wand
While you in white painter's pants adored
A sunflower, hoping it would shit across the nation.

The explosion taught us to read again.
Do not remember why everything is unsavory
That in the night a pineapple came
For this poster is nominally a conjecture.

DISTANT RELATIVES

Six o'clock. The fast fragrance
Is clawing past me, frantic to be let out,
Not competent to stand trial.

Like trees on a golf course
These hours propose themselves, one by one,
And each comes to terms with roundness.
The bobbed heads bob. The silence
For once is melony, sweet as the light
Off parked cars.

I don't need one of the hand-held jobs,
A heavy machine will do. And I must put across
Right now my idea of what it will do for me, before
It too founders in the tolling of leaves
(If all the tongues of all the bells
In this city fluttered silently)

As in that movie we saw where Mouloudji . . .

What will he do with it?
1. I don't get it.
2. It may not be worth it.

However the distances, it so happens, come to seem
Like partitions, both near and far:
Near, starting where my shoe is, and far
Ahead in the perspective, but connected
As the hours are connected to minutes
And I still feel the absence of you
As a thing that is both negative and positive
Like the broken mould of a lost
Statue
As the din becomes an uproar.

HISTOIRE UNIVERSELLE

As though founded by some weird religious sect
It is a paper disk, partially lit up from behind
With testaments to its cragginess, many of them
Illegible, covering most of its surface. In the hours
Between midnight and 4 A.M. it assumes a fitful
But calm sedentary existence, and it is then that
You may reach in and take out a name, any name,
And it will be your own, at least while
The walls of Bill's villa resonate with the intermittent,
Migraine-like drone of motorized gondolas and the distant
Murmur of cats. To be treated, at times like these,
To free speech is an aspect of the dream and of Dreamland
In general that asserts an even larger
View of the universe pinned on the midnight-blue
Backcloth of the universe that can't understand
Who all these people are, and about what
So much fuss is being made: it ignores its own entrails
And we love it even more for it until we too
Are parted like curtains across the empty stage of its
    memory.

The house was for living in,
So much was sure. But when the ways split
And we saw out over what was after all
Water and dawn, and prayed to the rocks
Overhead, and no answer was forthcoming,

It was then that the cosmic relaxer released us.
We were together on such a day. You, oddly
But becomingly dressed, pointed out that that
Day is today, the moral. All that.

HITTITE LULLABY

This time for you
The hair-blackened beans
And next semester the shouting
In carpeted corridors

More letters from the Sphinx
About what it was like

I greet you. I call to you
To release me from the contract
Morning flaps like a garment
Over a corner of the city

In mistrust with tears streaming
I can see clearly to know precisely
What is meant. My tact merely
A delaying stratagem
Is all I have. The sunlight
On your broad feet today
Withheld smiling.

Why did we board the ocean liner
Of lust signals out into the fog
Knowing there were excursions
But not this big one? My dog
Has died, I think. I come on you

All aspirations in the teeth
Of some pedantic ritual.
You take me where we were born.

IN A BOAT

Even when confronted by the small breakwater
That juts out from the pebbled shore of truth
You arch your eyebrows toward the daytime stars
And remind me, "This is how I was. This was the last

Part of me you were to know." And I can see the lot
Ending in the wood of general indifference to hostility
That wants to know how with two such people around
So much is finishing, so much rushing through the present.

There was a tag on the little sailboat
That idled there, all its sails rolled up
As tightly as umbrellas. What difference?
The orange shine stood off, just far enough away

Not to catch the commas and puns as you spoke
This time in defense of riders of the squall,
Of open-faced daring, not just to the empty seas
But for the people swathed in oilcloth on the beach.

"It is no great matter to take this in hand, convince
The tips of the trees they were rubbing against each other
All along. Each contrives to slip into his own hall of fame
And my common touch has triumphed. The doorpost shall
    turn again and again."

VARIATIONS ON AN ORIGINAL THEME

Our humblest destinies amount to this:
A maze of leaves, and one who sat
Within them dreaming of plants and their syrups
(Because of the yellow rings and zigzags
Visited on the moss-grown turret walls)
And a hare running far away, in the blond night.

And to dream of having sex with my beloved
Brings the figured wall no closer:
A fleet of pleasure boats and shadow
Dipping over them, lost
To the righteous eye brooding expensively
On tomorrow's fabric, how it overflows
Where there are no kick-pleats, and thins,
And what is wasted comes back anyway.

A ride in common variety
Was all it ever got to be; there are no friends
To make it serve. Only sometimes, a promised
Stranger makes us see it in another light
As though we have been standing here always,
Lake to the right, and the house, a Manichaean
Presence between the two widely spaced trees
On the backed-up, rusted gold of the grass.

And setting out in the punt on a larger
Stream and returning just in time
For the oracle, these things had not yet
Begun to dream, and there was thus no questioning
Of them yet. What was one day to be
Removed itself as far as possible from scrutiny.
We got down to the business of preparing
For the night only to find it prepared
For us as a bride, a flag rolled in the darkness,
Now no longer comfort, a spirit only.

HOMESICKNESS

The deep water in the travel poster finds me
In the change as I was about to back away
From the idea of the comedy around us—
In the chairs. And you too knew how to do the job
Just right. Trumpets in the afternoon
And you first get down to business and
The barges disappear, one by one, up the river.
One of them must be saved for a pirate. But no,
The park continues. There is no space between the leaves.

Once when there was more furniture
It seemed we moved more freely not noticing things
Or ourselves: our relationships were wholly articulate
And direct. Now the air between them has thinned
So that breathing becomes a pleasure, an unconscious act.

Then when you had finished talking about the trip
You had planned, and how many days you were to be away
I was looking into the night forests as I held
The receiver to my ear, replying correctly
As I always do, to everything, having become the sleeper in
  you.

It no longer mattered that I didn't want you to go away,
That I wanted you to return as quickly as possible
To my house, not yours this time, except

This house is yours when we sleep in it.
And you will be chastised and purified
Once we are both inside the world's lean-to.
Our words will rise like cigarette smoke, straight to the stars.

THIS CONFIGURATION

This movie deals with the epidemic of the way we live now.
What an inane cardplayer. And the age may support it.
Each time the rumble of the age
Is an anthill in the distance.

As he slides the first rumpled card
Out of his dirty ruffled shirtfront the cartoon
Of the new age has begun its ascent
Around all of us like a gauze spiral staircase in which
Some stars have been imbedded.

It is the modern trumpets
Who decide the mood or tenor of this cross-section:
Of the people who get up in the morning,
Still half-asleep. That they shouldn't have fun.
But something scary will come
To get them anyway. You might as well linger
On verandas, enjoying life, knowing
The end is essentially unpredictable.
It might be soldiers
Marching all day, millions of them
Past this spot, like the lozenge pattern
Of these walls, like, finally, a kind of sleep.

Or it may be that we are ordinary people
With not unreasonable desires which we can satisfy

From time to time without causing cataclysms
That keep getting louder and more forceful instead of dying
away.

Or it may be that we and the other people
Confused with us on the sidewalk have entered
A moment of seeming to be natural, expected,
And we see ourselves at the moment we see them:
Figures of an afternoon, of a century they extended.

METAMORPHOSIS

The long project, its candling arm
Come over, shrinks into still-disparate darkness,
Its pleasaunce an urn. And for what term
Should I elect you, O marauding beast of
Self-consciousness? When it is you,
Around the clock, I stand next to and consult?
You without a breather? Testimonials
To its not enduring crispness notwithstanding,
You can take that out. It needs to be shaken in the light.

To be delivered again to its shining arm—
O farewell grief and welcome joy! Gosh! So
Unexpected too, with much else. Yet stay,
Say how we are to be delivered from the fair content
If all is in accord with the morning—no prisms out of
    order—
And the nutty context isn't just there on a page
But rolling toward you like a pig just over
The barges and light they conflict with against
The sweep of low-lying, cattle-sheared hills,
Our plight in progress. We can't stand the crevasses
In between sections of feeling, but knowing
They come once more is a blessed decoction—
Is their recessed cry.

The penchant for growing and giving
Has left us bereft, and intrigued, for behind the screen

Of whatever vanity he chose to skate on, it was
Us and our vigilance who outlined the act for us.
We were perhaps afraid, and less purposefully benevolent
Because the chair was placed outside, the chair
No one would come to sit in, except the storm,
If it ever came. No shame, meanwhile,
To sit in the hammock, or wherever straw was
To see it and acclaim the differences as they were born.

And we were drunk as flowers
That should someday be, or could be,
We weren't keeping track, but just then
It all turned the corner into a tiny want ad:
Someone with something to sell someone
And the stitches ceased to make sense.
They climb now, gravely, with each day's decline
Farther into the unmapped sky over the sunset
And prolong it indelicately. With maps and whips
You came eagerly, we were obedient, and then, just then
The real big dark business got abated, and I
Awoke stretched out on a ladder lying on the cold ground,
Too upset and confused to imagine how you
Had built the colossal staircase in my flesh that armies
Were using now, their command a curse
As all my living swept by, the flags curved with stars.

THEIR DAY

Each act of criticism is general
But, in cutting itself off from all the others,
Explicit enough.

We know how the criticism must be done
On a specific day of the week. Too much matters
About this day. Another day, and the criticism is thrown
   down
Like trash into a dim, dusty courtyard.

It will be built again. That's all the point
There is to it. And it is built,
In sunlight, this time. All look up to it.
It has changed. It is different. It is still
Cut off from all the other acts of criticism.
From this it draws a tragic strength. Its greatness.

They are constructing pleasure simultaneously
In an adjacent chamber
That occupies the same cube of space as the critic's study.
For this to be pleasure, it must also be called criticism.

It is the very expensive kind
That comes sealed in a bottle. It is music of the second
   night
That winds up as if to say: Well, you've had it,
And in doing so, you have it.

From these boxed perimeters
We issue forth irregularly. Sometimes in fear,
But mostly with no knowledge of knowing, only a general
But selective feeling that the world had to go on being good
   to us.
As long as we don't know that
We can live at the square corners of the streets.
The winter does what it can for its children.

A TONE POEM

It is no longer night. But there is a sameness
Of intention, all the same, in the ways
We address it, rude
Color of what an amazing world,
As it goes flat, or rubs off, and this
Is a marvel, we think, and are careful not to go past it.

But it is the same thing we are all seeing,
Our world. Go after it,
Go get it boy, says the man holding the stick.
Eat, says the hunger, and we plunge blindly in again,
Into the chamber behind the thought.
We can hear it, even think it, but can't get disentangled
   from our brains.
Here, I am holding the winning ticket. Over here.
But it is all the same color again, as though the climate
Dyed everything the same color. It's more practical,
Yet the landscape, those billboards, age as rapidly as before.

THE OTHER CINDY

A breeze came to the aid of that wilted day
Where we sat about fuming at projects
With the funds running out, and others
Too simple and unheard-of to create pressure that moment,

Though it was one of these, lurking in the off-guard
Secrecy of a mind like a magazine article, that kept
Proposing, slicing, disposing, a truant idea even
In that kingdom of the blind, that finally would have
Reined in the mad hunt, quietly, and kept us there,
Thinking, not especially dozing any more, until
The truth had revealed itself the way a natural-gas
Storage tank becomes very well known sometime after
Dawn has slipped in
And seems to have been visible all along
Like a canoe route across the great lake on whose shore
One is left trapped, grumbling not so much at bad luck as
Because only this one side of experience is ever revealed.
And that meant something.

Sure, there was more to it
And the haunted houses in those valleys wanted to
   congratulate
You on your immobility. Too often the adventurous acolyte
Drops permanently from sight in this beautiful country.

There is much to be said in favor of the danger of warding
   off danger
But if you ever want to return

Though it seems improbable on the face of it
You must master the huge retards and have faith in the slow
Blossoming of haystacks, stairways, walls of convolvulus,
Until the moon can do no more. Exhausted,
You get out of bed. Your project is completed
Though the experiment is a mess. Return the kit
In the smashed cardboard box to the bright, bland
Cities that gave rise to you, you know
The one with the big Woolworth's and postcard-blue sky.
The contest ends at midnight tonight
But you can submit again, and again.

NO, BUT I SEEN ONE
YOU KNOW YOU DON'T OWN

Only sometimes is the seam in the way
Of space broken and three schedules cross:
The seasonable cold raging to be pliant and tit
Of gold.

He walks backward on the conveyor belt
As the blue powder of the day is dismissed
And he might pull the switch that would release
The immobile Niagaras that hover in the background.

There is no need, finally,
To inspissate the corded torsades
Of his loon voice. The dragees arrive in fumes:
The reprisal spinning through the air
Like an incandescent boomerang
As small flowers spring up at the feet
Of the near beasts, and in the distance
The hills are shrouded like shoulders
Behind the definitive errand of this glance.

THE SHOWER

The water began to fall quite quickly
Just wanting to be friendly.
It's too macho, and the sides and the plains get worse.
What are you writing?
Thus incurring a note for the milkman
City unit buses pass through. A laborer
Dragging luggage after cashing the king and ace of
It sifted slowly along the map, trying the lips,
The defender's last trick.

Somewhere in the grotto it festered,
The summer was cast in a circle. Knots
There were to see, knot by knot
But almost as much as is your punishment again.
By ruffing the third club defender would be
Just a fat man in sunglasses
That knots caress, moving
Through shine—the uncle in the mirror—
As it is beginning again these are the proportions.

Instead the place,
Where we had been before, got tangled
Within us, forced
To break out so that no one knew
The stalks from the knot of pleasure
And it would be determined to happen again—

Said this, through rain and the shine
That comes after, so many opinions
And words later, so many dried tears
Loitering at the sun's school shade.

LANDSCAPEOPLE

Long desired, the journey is begun. The suppliants
Climb aboard the damaged carrousel:
Some have been hacked to death, one has learned
Some new thing, and all are touched
With the same blight, like a snowfall
Of moments as they are read back to the monitor
Which only projects.

        Some can decipher it,
The outline of an eddy that traced itself
Before moving on, yet its place had to be,
Such was the appetite of those times. A ring
Of places existed around the central one,
And of course these died away eventually.
Everything has turned out for the best,
The "eggs of the sun" have been returned anonymously,
And the new ways are as simple as the old ones,
Only more firmly anchored to the spectacle
Of the madness of the seasons as it unfolds
With iron-clad rigidity, filling the sky with light.
We began in an anonymous sensuality
And lived most of it out before the difference
Of time got in the way, filling up the margins of the days
With pictures of fruit, light, colors, music, and vines,
Until it ceases to be a problem.

THE SUN

The watermark said it was alone with us,
"To do your keeping and comparing." But there were bushes
On the horizon shaped like hearts, spades, clubs and
    diamonds.
They were considered
To belong to a second class, to which lower standards
Were applied, as called for in the original rule,
And these standards were now bent inward to become
The invariable law, to which exceptions
Were sometimes apposite, and they liked the new clime,

So bracing here on the indigo slopes
To which families of fathers and daughters have come
Summer after summer, decade after decade, and it never
    stops
Being refreshing. It is a sign of maturity,
This stationary innocence, and a proof
Of our slow, millennial growth, ring after ring
Just inside the bark. Yet we get along well without it.
Water boils more slowly, and then faster
At these altitudes, and slowness need never be something
To criticize, for it has an investment in its own weight,
Rare bird. We know we can never be anything but parallel
And proximate in our relations, but we are linked up
Anyway in the sun's equation, the house from which
It steals forth on occasion, pretending, isn't

It funny, to pass unnoticed, until the deeply shelving
Darker pastures project their own reflection
And are caught in history,

Transfixed, like caves against the sky
Or rotting spars sketched in phosphorus, for what we did.

THE PLURAL OF
"JACK-IN-THE-BOX"

How quiet the diversion stands
Beside my gate, and me all eager and no grace:
Until tomorrow with sifting hands
Uncode the sea that brought me to this place,
Discover people with changing face
But the way is wide over stubble and sands,
Wider and not too wide, as a dish in space
Is excellent, conforming to demands

Not yet formulated. Let certain trends
Believe us, and that way give chase
With hounds, and with the hare erase
All knowledge of its coming here. The lands
Are fewer now under the plain blue blanket whose
Birthday keeps them outside at the end.

A selection of books published by Penguin is listed on the following pages. For a complete list of books available from Penguin in the United States, write to Dept. DG, Penguin Books, 299 Murray Hill Parkway, East Rutherford, New Jersey 07073.

In Canada for a complete list of Penguin Books write to Penguin Books Canada Limited, 2801 John Street, Markham, Ontario L3R 1B4.

John Ashbery

SELF-PORTRAIT IN A CONVEX MIRROR

This book won the National Book Critics Circle Award in Poetry, the Pulitzer Prize, and the National Book Award in Poetry for 1975. "These new poems are major odes to the joy of imagining, to the mitigation of sameness. They have a clarity akin to radiance. In their exciting oscillations—between image and act, art and life—what lingers on, after their startlingness, is their truth. This is some of the most serious writing in, and of America today"—John Hollander. "John Ashbery's new book continues his astonishing explorations of places where no one has ever been; it is, again, an event in American poetry"—Donald Barthelme.

HOUSEBOAT DAYS

Houseboat Days is John Ashbery's first collection of poems since *Self-Portrait in a Convex Mirror*, and it is in every way as dazzlingly original, as moving, and as forceful as its predecessor. Thirty-nine poems, many of them never before published, attest again to his extraordinary powers and the unparalleled range of his style. "Mr. Ashbery belongs," a critic has written, "to everyone interested in poetry, or modern art, or just the possibility of change. He is the great original of his generation."

THREE POEMS

Three Poems is one of the most profoundly innovative poetical works yet written by an American. Meant by Ashbery as a kind of trilogy to be read in sequence, the three poems open with a spiritual awakening to earthly things. Then Ashbery moves into wry, quasi-dialectical language to tell a love story with cosmological overtones and concludes with a poem that consolidates and fleshes out the themes of the previous two, balancing them with the sometimes harsh facts of his own autobiography.

Pablo Neruda

MEMOIRS
Translated from the Spanish by Hardie St. Martin

Pablo Neruda led the busiest, most impassioned, most dedicated, and, it has been said, happiest of lives—and these exuberant memoirs capture it all. As intensely lyrical as his world-renowned poetry, they recreate his frontier childhood, his student years in Santiago, his diplomatic missions, his election as senator, his flight from the Chilean police, his 1952 homecoming, and his last years crowded with palms and laurels. Here, too, the reader will meet some of the century's most important artistic and political figures: García Lorca, César Vallejo, Rafael Alberti, Paul Eluard, Louis Aragon, Pablo Picasso, David Alfaro Siqueiros, Mahatma Gandhi, Jawaharlal Nehru, Mao Tse-tung, Fidel Castro, Che Guevara, and Salvador Allende, whose death, occurring as Neruda completed this book, is mourned in its final pages.

John Steinbeck

STEINBECK: A LIFE IN LETTERS
Edited by Elaine Steinbeck
and Robert Wallsten

Here is the life of John Steinbeck as revealed in his letters, most of which have never before been published. These letters are imbued with all the passion that Steinbeck brought to his other writing. The collection opens with his early years in California, when he said, "I think I shall write some very good books indeed." It continues through the work on his plays and novels ("We have a title at last. See how you like it. The Grapes of Wrath from Battle Hymn of the Republic.") and closes with a 1968 note, from Sag Harbor, that ends in mid-sentence. To Steinbeck, who hated the telephone, letter-writing was not only a preparation for work; it was also his most natural means of communicating his thoughts on people met and loved or hated; on marriage, women, and children; on the condition of the world; and on his own progress in learning his craft. Distilled from more than five thousand letters, this book portrays him as nothing else has and as nothing else ever could.

PENGUIN POETS

In Penguin Poets there is a wide range of volumes which encompasses selections from the work of individual poets and anthologies of British, American, and foreign poetry. Each volume is edited and introduced by a distinguished authority in the subject. A sampling of Penguin Poets titles includes:

BAUDELAIRE: SELECTED POEMS
tr. by Joanna Richardson
CONTEMPORARY AMERICAN POETRY
Donald Hall (Ed.)
ENGLISH AND AMERICAN SURREALIST POETRY
Edward B. Germain (Ed.)
GERARD MANLEY HOPKINS: POEMS AND PROSE
W. H. Gardner (Ed.)
THE METAPHYSICAL POETS
Helen Gardner (Ed.)
THE PENGUIN BOOK OF BALLADS
Geoffrey Grigson (Ed.)
THE PENGUIN BOOK OF CHINESE VERSE
tr. by Robert Kotewall and Norman L. Smith; A. R. Davis (Ed.)
THE PENGUIN BOOK OF FRENCH VERSE
Brian Woledge, Geoffrey Brereton, and Anthony Hartley (Eds.)
THE PENGUIN BOOK OF GERMAN VERSE
Leonard Forster (Ed.)
THE PENGUIN BOOK OF JAPANESE VERSE
tr. by Geoffrey Bownas and Anthony Thwaite
THE PENGUIN BOOK OF LOVE POETRY
Jon Stallworthy (Ed.)